STONING THE DEVIL OF WAR IN SUDAN

Rethinking the Chronicles
Resolving the Puzzles
Reversing the Cycles

Eltigani Ahmed, PhD

ISBN: 978-9914-49-832-5

First Edition: 2023

Copyediting by Wandering Words (www.wanderingwordsmedia.com)
Quality Audit by LENS (informlens@gmail.com)
Interior Design by Formatted Books (https://formattedbooks.com)
Covers Design by 100-Covers (www.100covers.com)

DEDICATION

To My Family:

Tamador, Arwa, Areej, Aiman, Muhannad, Mohamed

CONTENTS

LIST OF ABBREVIATIONS

Abbreviation	Definition
AGNP	Agile Government of National Programs
ANC	African National Congress
ASP	Afro-Shirazi Party
AU	African Union
ICC	International Criminal Court
DDRR	Disarmament, Demobilization, Rehabilitation, and Reintegration
EAC	East African Community
FAA	Forças Armadas Angolanas (Angolan Armed Forces)
FRELIMO	Frente de Libertação de Moçambique (Mozambique Liberation Front)
IDP	Internally Displaced Persons
IEBC	Independent Electoral and Boundaries Commission
IGAD	Intergovernmental Authority on Development
IJMC	Independent Joint Monitoring Commission

LAS	League of Arab States
MENA	Middle East and North Africa
MPLA	Movimento Popular de Libertação de Angola (People's Movement for the Liberation of Angola)
OAU	Organization of African Unity
NIF	National Islamic Front
RECs	Regional Economic Communities
RENAMO	Resistência Nacional Moçambicana (Mozambican National Resistance)
RPF	Rwandan Patriotic Front
RSF	Rapid Support Forces
RUF	Revolutionary United Front
SADC	South African Development Community
SAF	Sudanese Armed Forces
TANU	Tanganyika African National Union
TGNU	Transitional Government of National Unity
TJR	Truth, Justice, and Reconciliation
TJRC	Truth, Justice, and Reconciliation Commission
TRC	Truth and Reconciliation Commission
UNITA	União Nacional para a Independência Total de Angola (National Union for the Total Independence of Angola)
WAEMU	West African Economic and Monetary Union

INTRODUCTION

"Hey, what's going on in Sudan?"

As fighting erupted in Khartoum on April 15, 2023, many people posed this question while anxiously awaiting an answer. Those who relate to Sudan, Sudanese or not, would typically answer thus: "The Sudanese Armed Forces and the Rapid Support Forces are fighting. They destroyed Khartoum and displaced its population. International mediators are pushing for a ceasefire."

Well, is that a conclusive answer? What about the secession of South Sudan after 50 years of relentless fighting? What about the war in Darfur? What about the war in the Nuba Mountains and Blue Nile Region? What about the conflict on the Eastern Front? What about the various political protest movements in central and Northern Sudan? What about future wars, assuming the conflict between the Sudanese Armed Forces (SAF) and the Rapid Support Forces (RSF) will have ended in one way or another by the time you read this book? What caused this northeast African nation to be backsliding for 67 years while its neighbors persevered into fledgling economies and teenage democracies?

A viable answer to "what's going on in Sudan" cannot be attained without a deep understanding of the historical and sociocultural underpinnings of the wars there. Conflicts do not erupt out of the blue without a buildup of prior drivers and determinants. However, the case of Sudan is unique since the nation has persistently experienced internal wars from the dawn of independence to date.

There must be an elusive dragon hiding somewhere, which wakes now and then to cause havoc. Every time and every place the dragon rained fire, people ran to their arms and started fighting, blaming each other for the destruction. If the underlying causes—the dragons—are not discovered and uprooted, any current or future war will be no more than an episode in an endless series of conflicts. The Khartoum war between RSF and SAF is potentially only the tip of the iceberg. In this book, I dig deeper into the submerged parts of the iceberg and attempt to provide a more realistic and inclusive answer to what is going on in Sudan. I will then build on that answer to chart a path to enduring peace and a resilient future.

The war between SAF and RSF was fought in the streets of Khartoum. The graphic scenes of fighters from both sides rejoicing and shouting, *"Allahu Akbar"*—Arabic for "God is great"—when seeing the dismembered and mutilated bodies of their adversaries, the apparent nonchalance of ordinary citizens passing by charred bodies lying on the roadside, and the level of destruction of the civilian infrastructure, all tell a story that is deep and beyond the firepower of the guns. It goes beyond any stretch of the imagination to think of stray dogs devouring human bodies on the streets of a capital city, images that are usually only seen in apocalyptic Hollywood movies.

The stubbornness demonstrated by the warring parties perplexed everyone, including the United Nations

Secretary-General, and prompted UN Humanitarian Chief Martin Griffiths to describe it as "one of the most brutal kinds."[1] This goes beyond the willingness to fight.

Sudanese fought most of their wars since independence against fellow Sudanese. But quite interestingly, they fought under religious, separatist, nationalist, and interventionist slogans. They tried and exhausted all war pretexts and, with hindsight, declared them futile. If the Sudanese do not find a reason to come together and accept each other, they will always find a reason to fight each other. But what elements constitute this uniquely complex war and those fighting it?

This book proposes an answer to what's going on in Sudan, using a fresh approach that detaches from the narratives of historical facts to critically investigate what the narratives fall short of revealing. Any firefighting effort not targeting the fire base will not extinguish the fire. Likewise, any peace effort not targeting the root cause of the problem is no more than palliative care. The book targets not the burning flames but the ignition faculties built into the source of the flame. Understanding the fire's intrinsic attributes helps contain its burning tendencies, regardless of the flame-proliferating conditions.

Stoning the Devil of War in Sudan was chosen as a title for this book to connote an attempt to break the serial and endless nature of the wars in Sudan. The Devil, also known as *Sheitan* (Satan), *Iblis*, or *Djinn*, is believed to be a fallen angel whom Almighty God (Allah, as known in Islam) cast down to Earth when he declined to prostrate before Adam in the glory of God of the Heavens.[2] Angels prostrated in obedience, and the Devil declined in arrogance.[3]

The Devil is made of fire, Angels are made of light, and Adam is created from clay.[4] The Devil is typically a metaphor for evil inclination.[4] The Devil vowed before God to derail humankind through temptation and apostasy. The Devil uses the power of *waswaas* (hypnotic seduction) to entice humans to evil.[5]

The name "Devil" symbolizes malicious temptation in the Sudanese culture. As overwhelmingly spiritual people, the Sudanese attribute evil deeds to the Devil. The expression *"Iqaf Sheitan Alharb"*—Arabic for "arresting or stopping the Devil of War"—is mouthed out occasionally when discussing efforts to end the war. The expression *"Ala'n Alsheitan"*—Arabic for "Curse the Devil"—is used to mean "be reasonable," "behave orderly," or "do the right thing."

This book adopted the title *Stoning the Devil* as a variant of "Cursing the Devil" to connote practical actions that lead to the divorce from evil acts, and sustenance of the path to orderliness. *Stoning* is practical, while "cursing" is verbal. Verbal actions do not transform people if not supported by practical ones. Leaders who act differently from what they preach are shadows of the Devil on Earth. *Stoning the Devil* means parting ways with the Devil through a commitment to exemplary behavior.

When Muslims go to Mecca for the annual *Hajj* (pilgrimage), they perform a significant ritual toward the end of their spiritual practice. The Hajjs (pilgrims) walk from the Mount of Arafat to Muzdalifah, where they spend the night collecting up to 70 pebbles each (or 49 pebbles for early leavers). The following four days, from 10 to 13 of *Dhul Hijjah*—the tenth day corresponding to *Aidul Adha Day,* or *"Youm Al-Nahr"*—they stone the Devil by symbolically pelting the three pillars at Mina with seven stones on the first day and 21 stones on each of the subsequent three days—known as *Days of Tashreeq.*

Stoning the Devil at Mina signifies Abrahamic tradition deeply enshrined in the Holy scriptures. Abraham saw in a dream that he was slaughtering his son. Dreams are one way God reveals messages to prophets. Abraham was believed to have stoned the Devil at Mina when the Devil tried to tempt him to disobey the order of God. The three pillars at Mina symbolize the Devil, and the pelting exercise symbolizes rebuking the Devil. In fact, they verbally rebuke the Devil at each throw of pebble.

The stoning of the Devil symbolizes an unequivocal declaration that the pilgrim is eternally separated from the Devil and all devilish deeds. After they stone the Devil (to death) and walk around the *Ka'bah* (the Holy Mosque), the pilgrims shave or trim their hair to signify being born-again Muslims. For a pilgrim, that day means a new dawn in life. That day should epitomize transformation, purification, and forever extinction of evil inclinations within one's spirit.

In a way, the book has adopted the title to signify the transformation of the Sudanese from people capable of endlessly fighting and self-profiling along ethnic or religious divides into a nation able to live in peace with each other. Fire has persistently molded events in Sudan since independence, starting as minor, isolated conflicts and growing into a roaring inferno. The progression of conflicts symbolizes the birth and growth of the Devil to beget more Devils, ignite more fires, and cause more destruction.

The book's title is a metaphor for the possibility of the Sudanese ending the persistent and escalating nature of the conflict in Sudan by stoning the Devil to restrain his evil deeds and acts. It connotes the Sudanese persistence in addressing equity and justice issues, halting the progression of minor issues to significant social and economic crises. This book unpacks the root causes of the Sudanese problem and attempts to find an answer to why Sudan has been at a standstill for 67 years.[6]

The subtitles *"Rethinking the Chronicles, Resolving the Puzzles, Reversing the Cycles"* connote logical and chronological significance. The logical significance is that reversing the cycles of war begins with rethinking the narratives to admit the presence of a problem and then move on to decipher its intricacies by resolving its puzzles. It connotes a chronological sense in that the sequencing of the subtitles tacitly divides the book into three sections.

Section One, *"Rethinking the Chronicles,"* covers the first three chapters and deals with diagnostic or root-cause elements.

Chapter One unpacks Sudan's missed opportunities by examining its historical, geopolitical, and resource advantages. The purpose of this discussion is to prove the argument that Sudan's persistent wars and underdevelopment are not related to a lack of resources or any geopolitical or historical disadvantages.

Chapter Two digs deeper into people-related aspects to frame an objective diagnostic of sociopolitical, sociocultural, and socioeconomic aspects that are seen as counterproductive or counter-progressive from a societal point of view. The secondary objective of this discussion is to expose some elements considered taboo or perceived as politically inappropriate, yet are widely acknowledged in moments of self-trust. As we progress in the discussion, it becomes clear that some socially tolerated behavioral attributes may have contributed to the recurrency of conflicts and the persistence of wars.

Chapter Three extends the discussion by exploring the structural hindrances to peace and progress. It covers lack of capacity, inadequate social infrastructure, security threats, impunity of offenders, and resource constraints.

Section Two, *"Resolving the Puzzles,"* consists of Chapters Four and Five. It aims to revisit some doctrines, thinking patterns, and historically held axioms, which I hold must be revisited with a critical eye. This section also provides analytics of comparable geopolitical contexts from within Africa. The central themes discussed in these two chapters include the quest for national identity—Tanzania's Ujamaa, Kenya's Harambee, and Rwanda and South Africa's Ubuntu—and the recovery lessons from African countries that experienced similar episodes of political instability or social discomfort: Rwanda, Angola, Sierra Leone, Mozambique, and South Africa.

Section Three, *"Reversing the Cycles,"* covers the last two chapters—six and seven—and presents policy-oriented actions.

Chapter Six introduces practical actions to improve political leadership, secure equity in socioeconomic development, professionalize the security apparatus, improve the country's foreign relations, secure transitional justice, rebuild the social fabric, and transform the education system.

Chapter Seven proposes a recovery roadmap for Sudan and recommends immediate, intermediate, and long-term actions that policymakers can adopt, with some alterations in line with impending realities on the ground.

The book ends with two crucial policy tools: a framework for Sudan's transition and a proposed composition of an agile government for national programs.

I had an opportunity to understand the Sudanese norms and cultures, having served nine years in a job that allowed me to visit all parts of the country, interact with the locals, understand their cultures, and build social relations. I spent the last 18 years of my career as an expatriate. I lived in Burundi and Kenya, and I visited most of Africa. I kept inspecting and observing what I saw across Africa through comparative binoculars.

I moved to Khartoum on August 20, 2020, for an international assignment and left Khartoum on March 24, 2023, barely three weeks before the SAF-RSF armed conflict began on April 15, 2023. Those two-and-a-half years were an excellent occasion to follow the progression of events and witness the transition from close range.

Although I share my views and ideas widely across my networks, I felt the need to contribute more to help bring lasting peace to Sudan. Any such contribution will have no value if driven by biased judgment or used for partisan propaganda.

If there were a single positive aspect of the SAF-RSF's destructive war, it would be that it woke up the conscience of the Sudanese and prompted them to ask tough questions about their identity and future. Therefore, I offer this book as an intellectual attempt to draw a roadmap for policymakers to address Sudan's problem sustainably. I attempt to objectively diagnose why Sudan fell far behind many countries in the region despite being on the first list of emancipated countries.

As with all diagnostic assessments, differing views and interpretations will always exist. Only a healthy intellectual discourse away from bigotry and profiling will lead to a logical diagnosis and sustainable treatment of the problem. In a way, this book calls upon all the Sudanese to ask the unavoidable questions, "What brought us to where we are, and where do we go from here?"

To this end, the book contains entirely neutral material from cover to cover. The thoughts and ideas, whether based on personal observation or borrowed from a source, are corroboratory facts verifiable through independent sources. For this reason, the book refers to all parties by the names with which they call themselves. No adjectives or name-calling describe any person or party in this book.

Furthermore, the book ignores controversial facts, statements, or descriptions that different parties may interpret differently. This book does not qualify, correct, or invalidate historical incidents. It only reports incidents and facts as known and reported at the time of their happening.

I have condensed the book for a pleasurable reading and packed it only with information I perceived as relevant for the reader to comprehend Sudan's problem quickly. The book is, therefore, relevant for policymakers, executives, politicians, diplomats, international organizations, academics, and anyone who seeks to know about Sudan and understand the dynamics of the Sudanese wars, including the latest one.

I intentionally avoided history recounting and picked events based on their relevance to the wars in Sudan. I supplemented this potential shortcoming with a wealth of resources at the end of the book for those who want to read more. I also adopted a straightforward writing style and used a casual tone to suit the general reader. Accordingly, user discretion, contextual judgment, and author disclaimers should be observed when citing or referencing this book.

Chapter One

RETHINKING THE MISSED OPPORTUNITIES CHRONICLE

Introduction

Most observers and analysts familiar with Sudan will agree that the country has the requisite ingredients to become one of the great countries in Africa in terms of political stability and economic performance. Sudan does not lack material or human resources and is strategically located, connecting Africa to the Arab world. Paradoxically, Sudan failed to tap into its immense resources to develop its economy.

Sudan has not experienced political stability since the dawn of independence in 1956. Countries cannot progress economically in such conditions. The repetitive nature of localized conflicts that gradually expanded to cover most of the Sudanese land tells a story of people seemingly unable to tolerate their differences and accept each other. The secession of South Sudan was clear evidence of this inability. Yet, the causes that allegedly prompted 98 percent of Southerners to vote "yes" for independence on January 9, 2011, may lead to further disintegration of other areas if not addressed sustainably.

Sudan has a rich history, abundant resources, intelligent people, and a strategic geopolitical location. In short, Sudan holds all the ingredients that make up a great country. In this chapter, I briefly look into these elements to build a case for my argument that Sudan's lack of progress is unrelated to resource poverty.

Political Image of the Recent Sudan

Sudan obtained independence on January 1, 1956. The period leading up to independence was marked by a wave of nationalism and the birth of two principal political parties, the National Unionist Party and the Umma Party, as well as several other smaller parties.[7] Sudan's political discord commenced right before its independence, when the elites self-divided along ethnic and ideological lines, making it difficult to agree on how the country should be ruled. It was apparent from the beginning that the question bothering the elites was *who* should rule the country and not *how* it should be ruled. This discord represented one of the most significant missed opportunities to begin self-governance on a positive note.

Sudan's immediate post-independent periods generated a positive aura on foreign and diplomatic fronts and produced historic moments of pride in Africa and the Arab world. In football, the first Africa Cup of Nations was held in Khartoum in 1957, and Sudan played the final against

Egypt. The first president of the African Development Bank was Sudanese, Mr. Mamoun Beheiry. The fourth and most critical Arab League Summit, known as "The Summit of the Three No's"—no peace with Israel, no recognition of Israel, and no negotiations with Israel—was held in Khartoum in 1967 in the aftermath of the defeat of the Arabs by Israel in the Six-Day War. Sudan also catalyzed the Organization of African Unity (OAU) in Addis Ababa in 1963 as one of the leading countries of the African emancipation drive.

On the low side, Sudan seemed to have been the victim of its success. It has been sedated by the historical triumphs and developed apathy, taking a back seat. It was contented to enjoy past glories and savor the taste of pride while other nations worked hard to catch up with the Africa-wide progress.

Despite a rich resource base, adequate infrastructure, and cultural diversity, Sudan progressively degenerated into internal wars. The continued political discord and the inability to agree on a bottom-line national agenda resulted in Sudan's first military coup, marking a political transition from democracy to military rule when the army commander, General Ibrahim Abboud, overthrew the government of Prime Minister Abdullah Khalil—a coalition of Umma and Democratic Unionist Party—in 1958, barely two years after independence.[8] The military coup was a tacit initiative of some politicians who invited or convinced the army commander to take over.[8] This change represented absolute precedent, proving that the elites could not lead the country's democratic process.

This first post-independence military coup marked the moment when Sudan's regressive trend began. For the next 67 years, Sudan kept recycling the same episode: a strong man from the army overthrowing a weak and divided democratic government, with the coup often inspired and backed by civilians or ideologized units within the army. General Ibrahim Abboud was ousted by the first popular uprising in 1964—known as Intifada. Democratic elections were held in 1965, won by the Umma Party of the late Prime Minister Al-Sadiq Al-Mahdi.[8]

In 1969, General Numeiri led another transition from democracy to military rule. Again, a coalition of left-wing political parties—*Nasiries* (pro-Egypt), *Baathis* (pro-Iraq), and Communists (pro-Soviet Union)—were behind Numeiri's transition. General Numeiri ruled until he was ousted by the second Intifada in 1985.[9] The 1985 Intifada was reproduced in the 2019 uprising. For comparison, the army led by General Suar Al-Dhahab backed the civilian protestors in 1985. It assisted in forming a transitional government that ended in elections won by the late Prime Minister Al-Sadiq Al-Mahdi's Umma Party, while in 2019, the army led by General Al-Burhan backed the civilian protestors and assisted in forming a transitional government under Prime Minister Hamdok that fell short of transitioning into democracy.[9]

In 1989, President Omar Al-Bashir orchestrated a transition from democracy to military rule, ending Al-Sadiq Al-Mahdi's civilian government. Al-Bashir's regime was incubated by the National Islamic Front (NIF) led by Hassan Al-Turabi.[10]

In 2019, Al-Bashir's 30-year reign was ended by the third Intifada.[11] However, the partnership between the army and the civilians that ensued from this transition did not work for several reasons—the most critical one, in my view, was continued discord among various political factions about who should rule. Instead of focusing on transforming the country into stability and prosperity, the transitional government was burdened by prolonged internal disagreements while the spirit of the revolution was overlooked.

The transitional government under Prime Minister Hamdok succeeded in improving Sudan's foreign relations, securing promises of debt forgiveness, stabilizing the exchange rate of the local currency, and initiating practical steps toward social peace.[11] These successes momentarily evaporated when the transition collapsed. Soon after, demonstrations resumed with full force, and Sudan regressed to political instability. What made matters worse that time was the invisible undercurrent of discord between and within various factions: military-military, military-civilian, and civilian-civilian.

A deep wound had been hastily stitched without proper dressing, leaving the infection to spread while the patient kept hiding the pain and smiling in front of cameras. It was only a matter of time before the wound exploded, throwing serous fluid into the open air. However, those who followed the events closely knew that the patient was in pain and may have predicted what was coming.

Regional Geopolitical Primacy

Sudan enjoys a strategic geographical position in the heart of Africa, connecting the continent from north to south and east to west. Before the secession of the south, Sudan shared borders with eight countries. After independence of the south, Sudan still shares borders with seven countries:

Egypt, Ethiopia, Chad, South Sudan, Central African Republic, Libya, and Eritrea. Sudan is also near the Middle East and North Africa (MENA), making it an ideal junction between Africa and the Arab world. Its cultural diversity and ethnic versatility are added advantages, making it an enviable melting pot for Arab and African cultures.[12]

The seven countries bordering Sudan collectively account for more than 30 percent of the African population, providing an extensive market of more than 400 million people.[13] If Sudan develops a sustainable trade exchange only with its neighboring countries, that may be adequate to sustain its economic performance.

Sudan opens to the Red Sea with a long coastline. The portion of the Red Sea near Sudan has the added advantage of deep waters and leveled underwater topography, making it ideal for constructing large-scale, multipurpose seaports and military bases.[14] Ethiopia has a population of more than 100 million and is a landlocked country that could rely on Sudan for port access in exchange for trade and strategic alliances.[15] Egypt has an equally large population and relies heavily on water from the River Nile, which flows through Sudan, providing an opportunity for Sudan to leverage it for a strategic relationship with Egypt based on mutual interests.[16]

The next regional conflicts are predicted to be primarily driven by disputes around natural resources, including water. The precursor of such conflicts is evidenced in the dispute between Ethiopia and Egypt following the construction of the Ethiopian Renaissance Dam.[17] Sudan's stance on this conflict should be carefully weighed based on net economic benefits to its people rather than emotion-driven political stances meant to please either party. The British statesperson Lord Palmerston is believed to have once said: "There are no permanent enemies, and no permanent friends, only permanent interests."[18] Politics is a game of possibilities, albeit possibilities that must espouse strategic interests of the countries involved.

South Sudan became an independent state in 2011 and started on a clean slate, with an urgent need for infrastructure development. Sudan could have used its proximity and technical knowledge to invest in the development of South Sudan.[19] The two nations have substantial historical and cultural ties, and therefore, South Sudan should not have been left languishing without support and pushed to look elsewhere. Ideally, South Sudan should not have seceded from Sudan for strategic intents, but since this has become a reality, Sudan could have maintained the status of a good and supportive neighbor. Politicians in the north failed to play this role and left the vacuum to be filled by other nations. Later in this book, I discuss this in more detail and recommend steps toward integrating the two Sudans with mutually rewarding strategic alliances.

Sudan shares a long border with Chad, and the two countries have several commonalities, including cross-border family ties, cultural similarity, and economic interests, such as livestock trading. Chad represents Sudan's bridge to the Francophone and Anglophone West Africa: Niger, Cameroon, and Nigeria. Sudan and Chad jointly share a strategic trade point with Libya, commonly known as "*Muthalath,*" or "triangle" in Arabic. Instead of developing this strategic point into a trade hub, it became a smuggling corridor for stolen vehicles and a transition for those adventuring on the perilous journey to Europe through the Libyan deserts and the Mediterranean Sea.[20] The three countries could not develop this tremendous geographical advantage into a trading hub—potentially because of political instability, but I think it is also partially because of a lack of leadership vision.

Like Chad, Eritrea also shares a border and culture with Sudan. The ethnic groups inhabiting eastern Sudan are culturally related to the ethnic groups in Eritrea, hold family ties on both sides of the border, and speak the same language. Eritrea has ports on the Red Sea (Assab and Massawa). This is an excellent opportunity to synergize with Sudan's ports for loading, handling, and transporting goods into the rest of Africa.[21] Most African countries neighboring the two ports are landlocked and can benefit immensely from such an opportunity if the ports were to be connected with cross-border rails. For instance, the two countries could develop joint ventures for rails, air freight cargo specializing in perishable goods, and truck routes into Ethiopia, South Sudan, the Democratic Republic of Congo, Rwanda, and Burundi. Increasingly, Rwanda and Burundi rely on the Dar-es-Salaam and Mombasa ports, where goods are transferred via trucks.[22] These routes are long and insecure, making them less viable than rail.

Sudan's geographic location qualifies it as a regional trade hub in this part of Africa. There are various elements of strategic synergies that Sudan could build with other regional hubs, such as Kenya and Djibouti. For instance, Djibouti has the advantage of being situated at the entry point to the Red Sea and the Gulf of Aden, and it serves as a link to the Indian Ocean.[21] Djibouti has gained relative strategic primacy from the international military bases hosted in the country to counter the various naval threats affecting the flow of international trade. The strategic intent of Djibouti is partially linked to the political instability in Somalia.[23] Nevertheless, Djibouti can sustain its geographic relevance by fostering collaboration with Sudan to gain market access to the countries neighboring Sudan.

Sudan's geographic advantage of being connected to seven African countries and in proximity to Western, Central, and Northern Africa—in addition to its sheer population size—makes it an attractive partner to Djibouti. I am not suggesting that Sudan will replace Djibouti in this respect, but I am alluding to the fact that Sudan and Djibouti can complement each other through strategic synergies. Both countries are culturally harmonized and can build win-win, collaborative endeavors.

Kenya has made progress in developing its infrastructure and has positioned itself as an economic powerhouse within East Africa. Its Mombasa port serves as a gateway into several landlocked countries. The port of Mombasa serves Uganda, the eastern Democratic Republic of Congo, South Sudan, Burundi, and Rwanda.[24] Like Djibouti, Sudan and Kenya can develop mutually rewarding trade relations in complementarity between Mombasa Port and Port-Sudan to serve South Sudan, the eastern Democratic Republic of Congo, Uganda, and the Central African Republic. Both Sudan and Kenya have rail and aviation infrastructure that can be combined with port infrastructure to develop full-service trade logistics.

International trade has become more competitive in recent years, and options windows are narrowing for

Africa. Part of the exceptional economic growth achieved by Southeast Asian countries was attributed to their enormous investment in trade infrastructure.[25] African countries have more pressing priorities and challenges and, therefore, do not possess the financial resources to compete with giants such as China, Singapore, and Thailand. The best alternative for African countries is to join hands in building cross-border and beyond-border trade facilitation logistics.

Europe has unified into the European Union through trade.[26] The West African Economic and Monetary Union (WAEMU) has similarly gone far toward economic integration.[27] The South African Development Community (SADC) is not far behind West Africa.[28] The Greater East Africa should push in the same direction. The East African Community (EAC) has organs that are already operational. This includes the Intergovernmental Authority on Development (IGAD) and the EAC. These can constitute a good platform for East African integration toward a greater United Africa that unifies all the Regional Economic Communities (RECs) into a single Pan-African economic and political powerhouse.

Let us not forget that Sudan is also a founding member of the League of Arab States (LAS). As such, Sudan is poised to play a pivotal role in increasing trade partnerships between Africa and Arab countries. Arab countries are net exporters of oil, and some countries have moved toward specialization on specific commodities and services such as agricultural inputs (Morocco, Algeria, and Tunisia), petrochemical derivatives (Saudi Arabia, Qatar, United Arab Emirates, and Oman), and medicine and pharmaceutical products (Egypt and Jordan).

On the other hand, most African countries still rely on exports of raw commodities (cashew nuts, cocoa, tea, gum arabic, cotton, and extractive minerals).[29] Some Arab countries, such as Saudi Arabia, UAE, Bahrain, Egypt, and Qatar, have developed intermediate technologies through origination or re-export from the Americas, Europe, and Asia. There is enormous potential for deepening trade complementarity between Arab and African countries in value-additive industries and supply of industrialization inputs, to name just a few. Sudan is at the center of this. This is an opportunity for Sudanese leaders to think ahead with vision and to convert these possibilities into realities.

Enviable Resource Endowment

Sudan is a fascinating country with breathtaking landscapes and diverse ecosystems. It holds within its borders an abundance of natural treasures, including fertile land, untapped mineral-rich underground, and boundless energy of renewable resources.[30] Sudan is known for being one of the wealthiest countries in Africa in terms of mineral potential. Its vast landmass and ecological diversity host various precious and base minerals, most of which are untapped.[30]

Sudan has substantial gold deposits throughout the north, south, west, and east. Numerous large-scale gold-producing ventures exist and have been long operational in Sudan, such as Hassai Gold Mines, Ariab Gold Mines, and Jebel Amer Gold Mines, but a great deal of gold is also extracted through artisanal mining, particularly in the north.[31] Estimates put the annual production of gold at

100 to 140 tons, of which only 30 tons are exported through official channels. The rest is traded unofficially.[31]

A country can sell gold to generate foreign exchange reserves to support current expenditure or keep it to bolster its gold reserves for future expenditure. Most countries stock gold to bolster their reserves. Selling gold to support imports is acceptable, but smuggling gold abroad is unacceptable. Smuggled gold is a loss of income and tax on future generations.[31] It compounds poverty in the long term because future income-generating potential is sold in advance and at a discount to foreign nationals. The proceeds of smuggled gold are used to develop economies and create job opportunities, but only in other countries.

Simply put, smuggling gold is tantamount to losing foreign exchange reserves or smuggling hard currency outside the country. It directly impacts the country's external position negatively. Smuggling gold is national treason and economic war on the country. Therefore, stringent laws and regulations should be adopted to deal with this malady.

Sudan also has commercial metals and minerals besides oil reserves.[31] For instance, Sudan has commercial deposits of copper around the Red Sea Hills and Nuba Mountains yet to be explored. In addition to copper and gold, Sudan has zinc, lead, chromite, manganese, gypsum, and limestone.[32]

Across Sudan's expansive territories, nature has blessed it with abundant renewable energy sources. Bathed in the radiance of relentless sunlight, Sudan is ideal for harnessing the boundless potential of solar power generation. In certain regions, fierce winds whisper of untapped wind energy opportunities, inviting the pursuit of renewable energy projects. Moreover, the Nile River and its tributaries offer a gateway to harnessing hydropower, ensuring Sudan's growing energy demands are met while embracing cleaner and greener energy alternatives.[33]

Agriculture is vital in providing nutrients and ensuring food security for Sudan. Fondly known as the "food basket of the world," Sudan has expansive fertile land with favorable crop growth conditions.[34] Sorghum—a cherished dietary staple—holds immense value within the country and has significant potential for international trade. Sudan can easily achieve self-sufficiency in food production and export to the rest of the world.

In addition to sorghum, Sudan produces one of the best cotton brands in the world. Its cotton fetched high premiums in the international market during the 1980s and early 90s, though cotton was later replaced with food crops to satisfy local demand.[34] Sudan also produces 70 percent of the world's gum arabic.[35] Unfortunately, most of the gum produced is smuggled out of the country. Besides smuggling, the sector has not seen the introduction of modern farming and extraction techniques and was left in bad shape, contributing to its persistent underdevelopment for decades.[34]

Over 70 percent of Sudan's freshwater sources are estimated to come from the Nile River.[33] It is the longest river in Africa and one of the most critical sources of fresh water for Sudan and many other African countries.[33] The Nile crosses nearly 7000 kilometers and covers 11 countries.

The 1959 Nile Water Agreement allocated only around 19 billion cubic meters for Sudan out of the Nile's 80 billion cubic meters, with the rest flowing to Egypt.[36] The river is fed by two primary sources: the Blue Nile, which originates from the Ethiopian heights, and the White Nile, which flows from Lake Victoria in Uganda. The river feeds from several tributaries, such as the Dinder River, Sobat River, Atbara River, and other seasonal streams known locally as *wadi,* or *wadies* in the plural.[33] The most notable ones are Gash and Baraka. These *wadies* are critical for the subsistence of the local communities.[37]

The climatic variability in Sudan is a source of rich ecological diversity. Heavy downpours characterize the country's southern parts. As you move northward, rains diminish, and the River Nile replaces seasonal rains as the primary aquatic source, particularly toward the borders with Egypt. [37] The southern parts are temperate, with less heat generating less evaporation and increasing surface water surplus.

Lands of the central and northern parts are more fertile, leading to higher crop yield, especially in the area of Al-Gadaref (toward the Ethiopian border) and Gezira in the Central Region (150 kilometers from Khartoum). These two locations host the largest cultivated areas in Sudan.[37] Sudan has several natural freshwater lakes, including Kundi in Darfur and Abyad and Al-Rahad in Kordofan. Sudan also has saline lakes, such as the Deriba crater in Jebel Marra and Malha in north Darfur, besides Nikheila, Natroon, and Saleema oases in the north. Groundwater is more readily available than other water resources during the dry season. [37] Sudan's enchanting forests cloak a sizable portion of its vast landscape, harboring invaluable resources and fostering biodiversity.

Within these verdant realms, precious timber, non-timber forest products, and the remarkable capacity for carbon sequestration lie waiting to be commercially exploited.[38] Sudan's forests support a rich tapestry of unique flora and fauna. Safeguarding these precious ecosystems and practicing sustainable forest management is paramount to preserving Sudan's natural heritage and nurturing the potential for ecotourism and carbon offset initiatives.[38]

Conclusion

Despite having all the elements of a great nation, Sudan failed to exploit its rich human and natural resource potential to be at least on par with its neighbors in terms of economic development and political stability. A country with such a massive and diverse potential should not have regressed into poverty and instability for decades. What went wrong? Their efforts seem to have been directed at generating political discord instead of coming together to develop the country. Who should be blamed for this? I rephrase the question to who should *not* be blamed?

Political leaders failed when they spent their efforts fighting for political allegiances. Intellectuals failed as they either played no role or packed up and left the country to its fate. Technocrats failed when they did not deliver proper and courageous advice to politicians. Religious leaders failed when they used their words to support nepotism instead of providing impartial spiritual guidance. Ordinary citizens failed when they neglected to stand up for their rights and fight nepotism.

What must be done? Is this African country forever cursed to regression? Should Sudan ever emerge from poverty? While I reserve the answer to the first two questions for later sections of the book, my emphatic answer to the third question is immediate, and it is "yes." My answer is based on what I know about the Sudanese. Despite my belief in the possibility of progress, beyond the endless political upheaval that the country has experienced since independence, other elements may continue to beget repetitive failure.

My claim that Sudan will rise is conditioned upon people's determination to critically address some softer issues that have contributed, in one way or another, to the stalemate. My view is that the road to recovery begins with admitting historical mistakes. If the Sudanese fail again to courageously admit their mistakes and come together to build a healthy nation, I fear this degenerative spiral will persist and take the country down a potentially irreversible path.

The preceding discussion validates my argument that Sudan's lack of progress cannot be attributed to a lack of resources. The root cause of the instability and stagnation must lie elsewhere. Hence, in the next chapter, I will unpack some symptoms of the social, cultural, and economic facets of the problem to provide an objective diagnosis of Sudan's war chronicles.

My central argument is that war is only the visible beak of an underwater monster that comes and goes with the tide. To stop the war—to stop seeing the monster's beak—you must locate and neutralize the monster. I will try to identify the physiological attributes of this monster in the next chapter.

Chapter Two

RETHINKING THE CONFLICT RECURRENCY CHRONICLE

Introduction

Why did Sudan repeatedly fail to redress and catch up with its regional peers? I will attempt to contribute some answers to this question by conducting a diagnostic assessment of the situation based on my observations, interactions with various stakeholders, and perspectives from several sources.

Unfortunately, not much literature has been produced on Sudan in the last 30 years because the prevailing political conditions did not provide a conducive environment for free thinking and writing. There has been strict censorship of writing and restrictions on book distribution in the country. Those who wrote from the diaspora, such as the iconic Sudanese fiction writer Abdelaziz Baraka Sakin, could not distribute locally. Daily newspapers were closely monitored and frequently confiscated when found to have published materials considered politically or culturally inappropriate. This environment discouraged many from writing about Sudan.

In this chapter, I assess the elements that have contributed in one way or another to Sudan's lack of progress. I divide them into three categories: sociopolitical chronicles, sociocultural chronicles, and socioeconomic chronicles. I use the term "chronicles" here with intention. These are foundational and exploratory discussions upon which I erect more solid policy and practical conclusions in the later sections of this book. However, I adopted descriptive, diagnostic, and experimental approaches interchangeably due to the scarcity of documented research. Hence, "chronicles," in my view, is the most appropriate term to describe these elements. In this sense, "chronicles" may be exchanged for "narratives" or "diaries."

The sociopolitical chronicles include peaceful cohabitation challenges, poverty-induced social injustice, civil service politicization, and inefficacious work ethos.

The sociocultural chronicles include excessive musclism inclinations (read further on this term below), irrational household economics, and inadequate social etiquette.

The socioeconomic chronicles include a distorted education system, undersupplied social infrastructure, and destruction of prime institutions.

Some elements listed in this chapter have been cited as principal causes of the chronic wars and instability, while others may have contributed to the economic regression and political recession. These will become clearer from the discussion in the following chapters.

Sociopolitical Chronicles

- *Peaceful Cohabitation Challenges*

Is it an overstatement to say that the Sudanese struggled to live peacefully with one another since independence? By "Sudanese," I am not referring to the people but rather to the system of governance that reproduced repetitive wars, displacement, coups, and political discord. Sudanese people are very tolerant and accommodative. They love visitors and foreigners. They show unmatched generosity when they receive guests. They celebrate visitors by slaughtering goats or chickens and sharing their little space with these visitors. If you visit a Sudanese family, you may be a detainee of love.

The Sudanese failed to tolerate political differences. They failed to do so not as people but as a system. The first civil war began in 1955 with the Anyanya Movement in South Sudan demanding more autonomy and recognition for South Sudan. Recall that Sudan gained independence in 1956, so the Sudanese began fighting each other even before their independence. In other words, independence was no more than a temporary truce. The war ended in 1972 with the Addis Ababa Peace Agreement.

The second civil war erupted in 1983 between the Sudan People's Liberation Army/Movement (SPLA/M) and successive central governments. This war continued until 2005, when the late John Garang signed a comprehensive peace agreement with the Government of the National Congress Party.[39] The two wars collectively cost the country two million deaths, six million displacements, and over 10 billion dollars in direct and indirect economic losses.[40]

A remarkable aspect of Sudan's second civil war was the use of religion as a war slogan, which meant that the war was a zero-sum game. Anchoring political discord on religion is dangerous because it does not allow middle-ground solutions. Either you are with us, or you are an enemy of God. I understand faithful Islam is tolerant, as evidenced by its history and the numerous Muslim countries where Muslims, Christians, and Jews cohabite peacefully. Islam did not spread worldwide through violence but because the Muslim migrants demonstrated an excellent example of being orderly and role models of conduct.

The African Union (AU) mediated a peace agreement in the latest South Sudan war, but it was apparent that the two parties were not prepared to accept one another. The five-year transitional period that ensued from the peace deal was marred by continued discord, resulting in only one logical outcome: the independence of South Sudan in 2011.[39]

The Blue Nile and Nuba Mountains share geographic, demographic, ideological, and cultural similarities with South Sudan. Therefore, the two resistance movements that started in these regions fought alongside the ranks of SPLA/M for decades before forming their version of the movement, named SPLA/M north. The fact that the new movement preferred the retention of the root name—SPLA/M—meant that they intended to sustain an umbilical cord with the mother movement.

Unlike South Sudan, these two regions were not included in the 2011 referendum, but the peace agreement acknowledged their special status and offered them a reconciliatory option known as "Popular Consultation." For reasons beyond the scope of this book, Popular Consultation never took place, and soon after South Sudan's independence, fighting resumed with the two rebel movements—led by General Malik Agar for the Blue Nile and General Abdul Aziz Al-Hilu for the Nuba Mountains—leading to famine and displacement.[41]

In 2003, the hypothetical dragon, once again, rained fire on Darfur and led to intense fighting between local armed groups and the central government. Interestingly, the nucleus of the Darfur movements, known as the "Sudan Liberation Movement," was originally a splinter of South Sudan's SPLA/M. It was started by Daoud Yehia Bolad, a rank commander of SPLA/M, who led a battalion from Southern Sudan and started a movement in the Jebel Marra area of Darfur. Bolad was captured and eliminated by government forces.

Soon after the end of Bolad's movement, a more significant movement of exact origin led by Menni Arcua Minnawi from the Zaghawa ethnicity invaded the regional capital, Al-Fasher. Zaghawa is one of the largest ethnic groups in Darfur and Chad. Zaghawa is the ethnic group the late Chadian President Idriss Deby hails from.

During that same period, the government formed quasi-military groups to support the official armed forces. The quasi-military was tasked to conduct specific military operations to quell the rebellion. The war in Darfur resulted in over 500 thousand deaths and more than 2.8 million refugees and internally displaced persons (IDPs).[41]

Another resistance movement formed separately by the Beja Congress and Rashaida Free Lions, jointly known as Eastern Front, started an armed protest in the Red Sea and Kassala regions along the Sudan-Eritrea border. The Eastern

Front demanded a fair share of resources and development.
[42] The eastern Sudan resistance movement is one of the
oldest movements that has been largely peaceful.

Eastern Sudan is one of the most resource-rich areas
of the country and includes the main naval gates of Port-
Sudan, Sawakin (or Suakin), and the marine oil terminal
of Bashair. Eastern Sudan is also where the Al-Gadaref
area is located. Al-Gadaref produces 80 percent of Sudan's
sorghum and sesame.[43] Despite this, eastern Sudan is one
of the poorest areas in the country and has experienced long-
term underdevelopment, lack of education, and absence of
reliable health facilities.[44]

The inhabitants of eastern Sudan have historically been
stereotyped, discriminatorily, as simple and complacent. I
assess that those people—Beja, Rashaida, Beni Aamir, and
Hadandawa—had limited options in their underdeveloped
areas. Thus, they were confined to involuntary unemployment, marginal labor, and futile handiwork.

Besides these five significant wars and hotspots of violence,
there have been various sporadic movements, both armed and
unarmed, throughout the country. A common characteristic
in all the protest movements is that they took arms to fight
for justice and demanded a fairer share of resources and inclusion. I argue that the similarity of the objectives of those
movements, despite their geographical diversity, only points to
the incompetency of the central government in managing the
diversity of Sudan. It is a chronic ineffectiveness of the ruling
elites to build a unified nation-state in Sudan.[42]

Why did the elites fail to lead the creation of a
nation-state? It may be because they were in a constant
search for an identity themselves. The elites seemed to have

little belief in Sudanism as a viable identity (see Chapter Four for more on the Sudanism philosophy).[45] The Sudanese elites seemed to suffer from intellectual inferiority. I define "intellectual inferiority" as a subconscious preference for acquired ideas over inherited ones. It occurs when a person gets fascinated by an idea to the extent that one considers their inherited ideas inferior to the new ways of life.

In the case of Sudan, intellectual inferiority could have originated from the new way of life brought by the Egyptians and the British, who colonized the country.[45] The assumption here is that the education system introduced by the British did not encourage Sudanism but instead promoted the new, alien way of life.

The political parties formed before independence were, to a substantial extent, replicas of political practices existent in foreign jurisdictions. This could imply that the elites found comfort in the acquired traditions and systems and developed apathy toward putting in more effort to promote a homegrown culture.[19]

The modern Sudanese way of life was centered in the confluence of the Nile River, where the greater capital—Khartoum, Khartoum north, and Omdurman—is located. Khartoum became a brilliant metropolitan area and a center of excellence in education, healthcare, services, and culture. At the same time, the rest of Sudan was conspicuously neglected, including the north of Sudan, which some people claim is home to a considerable portion of the elites.[42] I counter this claim because it amounts to baseless profiling of the people of north Sudan as those who inequitably took the lion's share of Sudan's resources at the expense of other regions, which is invalid.

When the late John Garang visited north Sudan after the peace agreement, he is reported to have said to some fellow Sudanese from north Sudan: "I think the reason why you did not become guerrillas is that you do not have a jungle here in the north."[46] By "guerrilla," he was alluding to his movement that started guerrilla war in the jungles of the south.

The north of Sudan is one of the most underdeveloped areas, and most development projects funded by international partners are in other parts of Sudan. The north has not received a fair share of development projects, apart from a fruit processing plant in Karima besides the Merowe Dam, which was constructed during Omar Al-Bashir's government. But the Dam was constructed to provide electricity to the entire country. As such, it cannot be considered as exclusively a development project for the north. It is also not entirely accurate to state that most elites come from the north. Elites from other parts of Sudan have had opportunities to participate in successive governments in the highest constitutional positions but have not done much to develop their own constituencies, let alone other parts of Sudan. The Sudanese elites are Khartoum-centric.

The previous statement by the late John Garang could be a testimony of the underdevelopment from which Sudan suffered historically. This could also explain that the underdevelopment in the other parts of Sudan may not have been intentional, simply because of the inadequate resource management model implemented in Sudan since independence.

Khartoum's population grew from a quarter of a million in 1956 to over six million in 2023. The urban infrastructure of the capital city has not been proportionally expanded to accommodate this large number of inhabitants.[47] Those who live in Khartoum can tell you about the traffic congestion, lack of services, and the unbearable plight of waste management with frequent explosions of the urban sewerage systems inundating the city's roads and mixing with rainwater-filled potholes. Every rainy season is preceded by a beehive of activity, with residents barricading the riverbanks with sandbags, a process repeated endlessly instead of a one-off investment in durable drainage systems to put the matter to rest.

This semi-exponential growth is a testimony of convenience-driven exodus, where people moved to the capital city to look for education, work opportunities, medical care, and better life conditions in general. This exodus negatively impacted productivity in deserted locations, most of which are economic activity centers. This is a typical life cycle of capital cities in underdeveloped countries. Some countries with relative economic ease tend to move the capital city to a new location.[48]

In the case of Sudan, a forced reverse migration from the capital city seems to have been initiated by the war in the capital instead. This is unfortunate because, ideally, reverse migration from the capital to rural areas should have been incentivized by better opportunities in the rural areas, such as work or investment opportunities, reliable government services, and good social infrastructure, instead of war-enforced reverse migration. The following paragraphs show how this convenience-driven migration to Khartoum compounded the recent war's economic impact.

▪ *Poverty-Induced Social Injustice*

When the war broke out between SAF and RSF in Khartoum on April 15, 2023, another war erupted in parallel. This war was equally destructive and had a potentially longer-term impact, but it was one to which no one had paid attention. The side-war was fought by an army of utterly poor and deprived individuals, most of whom resided in the poverty belt around the capital city. Most fled war and poverty from Darfur, Blue Nile, the Nuba Mountains, and South Sudan. They resettled on the capital's outskirts, hoping for a better life, only to find that the host locations were no better than the places they left behind. Those masses of poor lived on one meal a day at best. They found no jobs or social protection and faced hunger and deprivation.

In contrast, they saw how the affluent classes lived with relative ease. The government does not have a well-established social safety net system or non-contributory framework to care for those who can't afford to live decently. The deformed tax regime and public revenue generation systems afforded the central government no meaningful fiscal space for generous social program expenditures. The limited fiscal space has further been compounded by increased government expenditure on security because of various internal and external threats. Over the years, the gap has widened between the rich and the poor with a semi-collapse of the middle class. The poverty and marginalization experienced by the IDPs living within Khartoum's poverty belt deepened the feeling of social unfairness from the point of view of the IDPs.

Thus, when the war broke out between SAF and RSF in the capital, an army of people experiencing poverty conducted another parallel war in their own way. Reports have come out of masses flooding from the poverty belt into the most affluent areas of Khartoum—Al-Amarat, Al-Riyadh, Taif, Kafoury, and Manshia—armed with tools to break into houses. They began looting anything they could, from TV sets to cookware. No neighborhood in Khartoum was spared from the looting, but the primary targets were the affluent locations because of the perception that the looters could stumble on precious items left behind by the fleeing residents.

Some reports linked armed groups with the looting spree, but the reports related them to the theft of precious items such as motor vehicles, gold, mobile handsets, and cash. Some claimed that armed groups broke into houses using weapons, while the battalion of deprived people intently marched behind them at carefully paced distance and timing to ransack the leftovers or break into intact houses using any equipment at their disposal.

Long-term deprivation creates an insatiable avidity that pushes a person to excessive intake or over-possession. The second-century BC Roman Republic practiced a form of capital punishment known as *damnatio ad bestias,* or condemnation to beasts, where sentenced persons—usually criminals and runaway slaves—were thrown to hungry lions who devoured them to the bone. At the same time, crowds ecstatically watched as if enjoying a sports game.[49] The cats were kept hungry in cages for days to ensure they spared no flesh from the victims.[50]

The point is that a ravenous beast overeats when they finally feed. Likewise, an extremely deprived person over-possesses when given a chance to possess, and a destitute person over-exposes their wealth when they get rich. Perhaps one could use this analogy to understand why some dictators left behind properties, jewelry, cars, and mansions worth billions of dollars when they died while their fellow citizens could not afford life-saving medicine.[51]

Some of those dictators may have experienced poverty in their childhood and, therefore, over-enriched when they found a chance to do so. Poverty and violence are entangled in a way. People experiencing poverty grow in violence, and when they become leaders, they exercise repression on their fellow subjects to compensate for what they experienced or missed in childhood.

Like the ravenous lions, armies of people experiencing poverty in Khartoum over-looted belongings left by those who had escaped. As a result of over-looting, some found themselves possessing excess items and attempted to exchange them for cash. However, due to a shortage of local currency caused by months of unpaid salaries and the banking system collapse, a strange discount market was developed where household items were sold for less than 10 percent of their market price.

Many factors contributed to the looters' openness to selling the stolen items at massive discounts. First, the items were stolen, so clearly, profit and loss principles were not applicable. Second, the looters wanted to get rid of the items as fast as possible to make money for living or to free up space for more looting. Third, there was no liquidity, so the easiest way to sell was through massive discounts. Fourth, getting rid of stolen items faster is an effortless way to avoid being caught.

I have been informed that most people did not buy items from those markets, but still, they flourished to some extent because what was supplied eventually found a buyer. The very existence of such markets reveals how deep the destruction of the social fabric is in Sudan.

I want to stress that stealing other people's property cannot be justified by poverty or any other social injustice. Those who steal do so not because they are poor but because of criminal tendencies. I have been talking to some victims of these thefts, and what they describe goes beyond stealing. It is as if the thieves steal for vengeance. They often leave nothing intact, vandalizing the windows and doors and deforming the trees and gardens. One person narrated how the thieves poured cement into toilets.

▪ *Politicized Civil Service*

Sudan has been in a cycle of democracy, coup, and democracy again for 67 years. Some political transition episodes were marked by laying off civil servants and appointing supporters to senior government positions. Apparently, political leaders at each transition wanted to guarantee the support of loyal civil servants to help them accomplish their political agenda and to reward them for their loyalty and support.[52]

The slogan "*Tat-Heer Qabl Al-Taameer*," which means "clean up before you build," has been the norm during some political transitions. This meant that selection for civil service positions was based primarily on allegiance rather than competence. Consequently, civil servants perceived not to be aligned with the political orientation were laid off en masse.

Civil service is sacred in most countries because it forms the basis of economic prosperity. The stability of civil service allows for the preservation, growth, and transition of knowledge and expertise across generations.[52] Frequent civil service changes do the opposite, especially when the old folks perceive the newcomers as being brought in to replace them. In such cases, the outgoing fellows have no incentive to transmit knowledge to the newcomers.[53]

In the case of Sudan, there has also been an observable trend of increased family-based favoritism in civil service.[53] Some political or armed protest movements cited inequality in civil service as one of the reasons for their uprising.[52]

Some Anglophone African countries inherited a reliable civil service tradition renowned for work protocol, strict time management, professionalism, respect for working hours, and dress code. Most countries preserved and transferred this tradition across generations, and this explains why civil service is efficient in countries like Uganda, Kenya, South Africa, Zimbabwe, Zambia, Ghana, and Malawi.

Sudan lost this tradition partially because of the reasons mentioned earlier. Although some institutions still maintain a few traditions, such as dress codes, most intrinsic values that enhance productivity are hardly perceivable. I spoke with a senior Sudanese who served in the 1970s and 80s. He reminisced over the good old days with palpable emotions: "We destroyed every good thing in this country." It is unclear exactly when Sudan's civil service began to degenerate, but the deterioration seems to have started in the late 1980s.[52]

■ *Inefficacious Work Ethos*

A glaring sign of the loss of direction for the youth is the number of young people spending several hours around ladies selling tea on roadsides, known as *"Sittat Alshai."* The young fellows would spend long hours chatting about everything except their future. Seeing young people playing cell phone Ludo games and smoking shisha—a molasses-based tobacco heated to vapor—cannot be missed in some parts of Khartoum. While having tea with friends is not out of the norm owing to how the Sudanese love tea, wasting unnecessarily long hours in tea gatherings leaves less time for an average person to take care of other essential life matters.

Take a quick visit to a high-end restaurant, upmarket shopping outlet, or an international hotel in Khartoum, and you cannot miss observing that they prefer hiring foreign nationals instead of Sudanese. Upmarket businesses intend to maintain service quality and, therefore, cannot employ people with a tendency for absenteeism or low performance. On the other hand, there is a noticeable growing trend of small businesses owned by foreigners while the Sudanese youth spend their time around *Sittat Alshai.*

Apathy to work is the second evidence of loss of direction. Some Sudanese are more productive when working abroad or locally for expatriates. However, when working for fellow Sudanese or managing their own business, it is an outright disaster, in most instances. Official working hours begin at 8 a.m., but most private businesses open at 9 or 10 a.m. No official law governs opening and closing hours for non-governmental businesses. Service venues open and close at will. Some business owners decide to close their premises for all sorts of reasons, including visiting a friend or relative in the hospital, attending a funeral, or simply when they do not want to go to work that day. No one holds them accountable for when they should open and close their businesses.

Opening hours should be visible at entrances and on various businesses' websites. In Nairobi, searching online is the easiest way to get routine services, such as a plumber to fix your water, a mechanic to repair your vehicle, or a property agent to help you find a flat. You search online, call the mobile number, and the service person is engaged in your service within a conveniently brief time. In Khartoum, finding a dependable service person is like looking for a needle in a haystack. If you are lucky to find one, you will likely end up paying twice—for the first attempt and the repair of the first attempt. There are a few instances where you get satisfactory service, but the general rule is a lack of perfection in professional services.

Government offices are not any better. While government officials must report from 8 a.m. to 4 p.m., their presence at work is flush with idleness. Again, there are no concrete statistics to account for the level of productivity of a Sudanese government official, but the general impression you get when visiting a government office is that people spend more time socializing and less time producing. People spend the first morning hour greeting each other and speaking about all matters, including a football match from the previous night. Next comes breakfast time from 10 a.m., which will be stretched to midday, with tea, coffee, and visiting friends.

At noon, people break for *Dhuhur* prayers. This is supposed to be a brief break, but some are eager to extend it with socializing, Holy Koran recitation, or lengthy staging at mosques. For clarity, there is nothing wrong with praying in a mosque or reciting the Holy Koran. Caring for people's needs is more spiritual and fundamental in Islam, particularly when the service is prepaid through salary earned. While the Koran can be recited at night, early morning, or late evening, people's needs are strictly time-sensitive when they visit government offices for services that they expect to be delivered with dedication. In my view, this has nothing to do with religious commitment but more so with personal integrity.

Integrity is an abstract human value, irrespective of a person's religion. It does not matter if you are Muslim, Christian, Jewish, Buddhist, or agnostic—if you have personal integrity, you have personal integrity. If you don't have it, you cannot hide behind religion. Taking deliberate, long prayer breaks while people are waiting in queues to be served is dishonesty; it is not different from spending office hours on social media and computer games. You are fully paid for the office hours but have not equally delivered your part of the deal. You have received a financial reward without corresponding effort. This behavior is known as short-changing, or "Tatfif," and those doing it are "Mutaffifin or Mutaffifoon, as known in the Holy Koran."

Short-changing is a form of free-rider behavior where a person gets their rights in full while absconding to their duties. The Holy Koran referred to short-changing in the context of trading exchanges where traders use fair bushels or scales when they are the buyers while using biased ones when they are the sellers. This action would guarantee them a fair trade while denying others equal rights. Nevertheless, the concept of short-changing has broader applications as it extends beyond trading to all dealings involving rights and duties. In that sense, if you ensure you get your rights fully while not paying equal attention to performing your duties for others, you are a short-changer or a *Mutaffif.* It is as simple as that. Short-changing is prevalent in most aspects of our social, political, and economic lives nowadays.

To make office hours productive, eating habits must change. Most Sudanese are not used to early morning breakfast. Instead, they have their first meal at 10 a.m., lunch at 4 or 5 p.m., and dinner at 8 p.m. If government officials report to work at 8 a.m., they should not break for breakfast at 10 a.m. They should have a light meal before getting to their offices.

Further, an official lunch and prayer break should be allowed. The current practice is that employees are required to work continually from 8 a.m. to 4 p.m. with no break. Since there is no official break, they create multiple breaks, reducing their productivity. To be precise, all the breaks mentioned above are not official. Hence, they are abused under various alibis.

Some friends told me about an increased insider-trading tendency whereby salaried officials seek rent for government services. That is, they make it extremely difficult for clients to obtain routine services through official means. Meanwhile, somehow, someone would hint to you that you could ease your way around by sliding an envelope under the table. Sometimes, they don't tell you frankly for fear of being reported, but you can sense it from their body language or the way they purposefully delay you. In other words, you have to pay a bribe to be served to your satisfaction. If you resist bribes, you may be targeted by torturous bureaucracies.

To make the long story short, Sudan's progress hinges on a complete revamp of the civil service. This could be done by hiring consultants with experience in similar situations to restructure government and private services, review the laws, and recommend that some counterproductive practices be abolished. For this to be done, a solid political will must prevail.

Sociocultural Chronicles

- *Inclinations for Excessive Musclism*

What is "musclism," and how can it relate to the recurrence of wars and instability in Sudan? I kept pondering an exact term I could use to describe the social conduct I observed, which I feel had something to do with repetitive wars in Sudan. Simply put, this behavior relates to people being more inclined or prepared to use physical advantage to navigate issues they face. I initially thought of "masculinism" and "masculism," but neither turned out pretty fitting. For the lack of a better word, I coined the term "musclism." I derived it from "muscle" to describe social conduct where men use overt power or physical appearance to gain an advantage or attract attention. It does not necessarily imply an inclination to physical violence, but rather that a man who demonstrates relative prowess commands respect in society. Prowess can include physical attributes, such as muscle and body size, but it can also refer to nonphysical advantages, such as voice, wealth, social background, or kinship with a prominent social, political, or military figure.

Physical prowess can be demonstrated in physical power, verbal prevalence to win an argument, and attachment to physical means of defense—sticks, knives, or firearms. One observable phenomenon in society is the increased number of young men carrying knives. Again, there are no reliable statistics on this observation, but it is noticeable, particularly in the peripheral neighborhoods of the capital city.

Attaching a knife to the body is a practice that is recognized and tolerated in some rural parts of Sudan, particularly in Darfur, Kordofan, and eastern Sudan, where men attach knives to their biceps or waist. The knives, covered in decorated leather cases strapped to men's biceps or other parts of the body, are seen as a sign of bravery and maturity. The migration of this culture to Khartoum is recent but requires some research to understand the underlying dynamics.

Knives and pistols are sandwiched in the waistline between the belt and pants, with the butt or magazine left intentionally nosing outward for deterrence. The law prohibits carrying unlicensed firearms and weapons, but no one seems to care about enforcing the law, rendering this phenomenon almost natural. It may well be that the level with which the recent war was battled and the indifference of ordinary citizens watching and sometimes tolerating violent scenes could somehow be related to musclism.

Sudan has been under military rule for 56 out of 76 years of self-governance since independence. The military is a place of discipline, order, and obedience.[54] But the military is also associated with force, punishment, and using the power of position to manage subordinates. In the military, you cannot use logic to negotiate your way around.[55]

The extended prevalence of military-style administration in Sudan seems to have transformed the society into large barracks where only the language of authority is understood. This is what society seems to have come to terms with. But more interestingly, the last 30 years of military rule have seen a wave of militarization of society through popular defense forces, popular police, popular intelligence, and compulsory military conscription. This is particularly the case for the youth under the "Izzatus-Sudan" military conscription program that was made mandatory for entry into higher education institutions. After graduation, every student must also spend two years in national service before being allowed to apply for a job. The long-term sanctions made matters worse for Sudan by isolating the country from the international community.[56]

One tends to believe that sanctions may have contributed to worsening Sudan's problems in one way or another. This may seem to be a loaded statement. However, the hidden cost of sanctions is the isolation of the country from the international community through travel restrictions, limited transfer of knowledge, less interaction with the global community in sports and cultural events, and the denigration of the status of the national passport. This has led the rest to view the Sudanese with a suspicious eye. 87

Some Sudanese who live and work abroad experience challenges opening bank accounts, participating in international conferences, and competing for international senior positions, even though they may be technically competent. In short, sanctions place the whole country under a veil, limiting the opportunities available for Sudanese youth and accentuating the localized mindset where youthful aspirations become limited to the local economy's opportunities.

Compare this to open economies, where youth make headlines for their great entrepreneurship ventures, tech startups, and global success in sports. This is made possible partly by frequent interaction with their peers globally and by developing a mindset open to learning and cultural exchange. Sudan has missed these opportunities because of sanctions and internal repression.

Based on this observation, one could argue that blanket sanctions on countries are not the best option to force countries to respect human rights or combat terrorism. Sanctions have not deterred countries from developing nuclear weapons. Sanctions did not improve human rights records. In most cases, sanctions did not result in regime change, as leaders targeted by sanctions encapsulate themselves in multiple layers of counter-defensive measures, leaving ordinary citizens to suffer from the economic burden of the sanctions.[57]

▪ *Irrational Household Economics*

The Sudanese are typecast for their generosity and honesty. But might that have gone a little overboard? Before discussing this, it should not be misunderstood that too much honesty is awful, or that too much generosity is an evil act. What should be understood is that there are boundaries to everything. When a thing crosses boundaries, it often passes through reason to the edge of the next boundary. Unmeasured generosity could be perceived as a form of naivety, especially when it involves reckless spending without being cautious enough to save a penny for rainy days.

The demarcation for each attribute is fairness. Fairness to life, to work, to relatives, and self. Self-fairness is the ultimate form of self-justice. Self-fairness should not be taken for self-love. Self-love may sometimes cross boundaries to selfishness, another manifestation of short-changing behavior discussed in the previous paragraphs. Self-fairness is a balancing act of treating oneself how you would treat others and treating others how you would want to be treated. You don't have to love a person to be fair to the person. Likewise, you don't have to love yourself to be fair to yourself.

One outright manifestation of self-fairness is self-discipline. This topic is extensive and cannot be contained in a single publication. However, it suffices to give a simple definition of self-discipline; in its simplest form, it means *inherent preparedness to submit to the rule of law and orderliness.* The rule of law is made to be respected, not broken. The rule of law serves its purpose only if it is respected. Sometimes, the rule of law is breached subconsciously with too much individual discretion.

No one should be offered the discretion to disrespect the rule of law. Respect for the rule of law is not by choice but by a social contract. When parents follow the rule of law, their children and grandchildren respect it, partially because they saw their parents do the same and partially because they have been convinced, and not forced, to do so. But when parents preach one thing and do precisely the opposite, children will be law-abiding citizens only when under watch. They will do it only out of fear. When parents are not on the watch, it is monkey business as usual. The parents' suitability as role models is conditional. What applies to children applies to adult citizens.

Disrespect of the rule of law begins with minor things, including the temptation to leave trash by the roadside. Some motorists litter on the move, especially on safaris. If you are on an upcountry drive and get the urge to roll down your window to throw an empty can or banana peel by the roadside, just the urge, then you know you are on the wrong side of the rule of law, even if that rule of law is unwritten. It means you are uncivilized. It means that what deters you is fear of punishment. That leads me to the second outright manifestation of self-fairness: sincerity.

What is being sincere? What crosses your mind when no one watches over your actions? Do you adopt a particular behavior to please others? Or do you adopt a behavior to satisfy yourself? Being sincere means your actions are driven by your desire to be the best version of yourself, no matter what. Being insincere means your actions and behaviors are driven by affectation. It means they are pretentious and intended to impress others, not yourself. Affectation is a social malady that converts social actions into empty pretensions that do not uplift society. Let us put this into context with an example.

One conspicuous example is herd-style extravagant spending on weddings, graduation ceremonies, complimentary household items, and seasonal festivities. A person may be prepared to forgo life necessities to spend their savings on house renovation, graduation, or acquiring a brand-new vehicle because a neighbor next door has just done the same. This herd-style behavior is rampant in society and driven by a desire to show off and maintain social status at the expense of living beyond their means. It is also sometimes driven by social or peer pressure to maintain a similar status with a neighbor, a friend, or a relative.

One interesting observation that caught my attention is the similarity between adjacent businesses. For instance, if you see a pharmacy, you will often see a second pharmacy steps away and a third one a few meters down the road. If you walk past a restaurant, I bet you will walk past a second restaurant steps away and another one after that. While this could be driven by healthy competition, which brings market efficiency, more often than not, it is because neighbors like copying each other to maintain similar social status or due to apathy in generating fresh ideas.

Judging by the size of the household economy and unemployment rate, particularly among the youth, the average Sudanese is a low-income person.[58] Within a typical household, only a few members have jobs, and the rest of the family depends on the principal breadwinner. Society is subconsciously tolerant of unemployment because of the typical generosity that distinguishes a Sudanese person, such that the working class would spend nearly their entire earnings on family and relatives. While this behavior connotes the spirit of solidarity on the face of it, it also promotes free-rider behavior—a form of moral hazard where a person lacks the incentive to look for a job because someone else is willing to provide for them unconditionally.

This means that household disposable income barely covers subsistence expenditure. Therefore, no household savings or wealth formation can be realized in such cases. In aggregate, if enough households earn little income and spend it all extravagantly, society will become poorer in the long term because extravagant expenditure is irreversible, meaning that money spent extravagantly cannot be redeemed. It's at a colossal discount if it can be redeemed at all. That society is not resilient enough to withstand economic shocks. The country will grow poorer, and the economy will languish.

Not being a rational economic agent at the household level manifests in how successive political regimes in Sudan were unsuccessful in exploiting the country's resources to develop a robust and broader base for economic growth. A societal behavior or political system conduct is an aggregation of the behaviors of the individuals constituting that society or political system. Therefore, how public affairs in a country are managed cannot be separated from how its constituents conduct their household affairs. Sudan is a resource-rich country that continues to be poor.[58] Sudan produced nearly 500 thousand barrels per day (bpd) of crude oil from 2005 until 2011. By then, the country had net foreign reserves covering at least seven months of imports.[59] The Oil Stabilization Account had sufficient balances in US dollars to revolutionize the agricultural sector.

Oil production and exports cursed the country more than they blessed it, because managers failed to plan proper expenditure of the oil revenues to spur long-term economic growth. Oil revenues should have been prioritized to grow the economic sectors where Sudan has a comparative advantage: cotton, gum arabic, and livestock. Instead, extravagant consumption patterns were developed, and the productive sectors were neglected.[59] This may not be entirely the government's responsibility. Technocrats are equally responsible for failing to develop and execute viable plans.

With its massive 2.3 million acres, the Gezira Scheme would produce enough cash crops to improve the country's trade balance. Sudan produces one of the best cotton brands in the world.[42] Because of the price differential, cotton generates more foreign exchange than wheat. Unfortunately, areas under cotton cultivation in Gezira were replaced with wheat to satisfy a political slogan termed: "*Naakul Mimma Nazraa Wa Nalbas Mimma Nasnaa,*" which loosely translates as: "We eat what we grow, and we wear what we weave."

The world economy is integrated. You don't have to misallocate resources—if you could produce and export cotton, you could use your export proceeds to import food. The world economy sustains growth through complementarity under resource endowment, comparative advantages, specialization, and trade. In the end, Sudan lost dominance of world cotton exports to West Africa and still covers a greater share of its domestic demand for wheat from imports.[42] In other words, the touted agricultural revolution cost the country its position as a cotton exporter while failing to achieve wheat self-sufficiency.

- *Inadequate Social Etiquette*

Nations cannot flourish without adopting orderliness in the way they go about their daily businesses. I was once on a flight from King Shaka International Airport Durban to OR Tambo International Airport Johannesburg with two fellows. The rest of the flight was packed with South Africans and a few other nationalities. When the Airlink's Embraer Jet landed at Tambo, no passengers except us attempted to leave their seats. Cognizant of our mistake and noticing that the whole aircraft's passengers were looking at us, we quietly but nervously returned to our seats and started conversing in Arabic. We thought something was wrong with the aircraft because no passenger reached up for their cabin luggage.

When, finally, the door opened, the business-class passengers exited one after the other in fantastic order, starting from the row closest to the exit. Next, economy passengers began exiting in the same orderly manner. I noticed that the next passenger would not reach for their luggage until the one ahead had taken all their belongings. The small aircraft was emptied with that same orderliness.

As we headed to the exit, one of my friends could not hide his frustration with *excessive* orderliness. He said he got nervous and developed an urge to pee. Aviation protocol requires passengers to remain seated until an aircraft stops and seatbelt signs are turned off.[60] As an aircraft touched down and while taxiing to park, a typical passenger already had cabin bags on their lap, cell phone powered up, and was making calls.

This could still be isolated incidents. The average Sudanese is calm and peaceful. Nevertheless, a noticeable trend of people being short-tempered and impatient has been growing. I usually notice passenger impatience on flights heading to Khartoum or leaving Khartoum, where passengers crowd the gate and elbow each other before the gate opens. One rare behavior I could not find justification for was when I saw economy-class passengers intentionally fill business-class cabin luggage compartments with their own bags before proceeding to their economy-class seats. I must admit, however, that I have also seen this behavior on other regional routes.

In contrast, other nations neighboring Sudan have an acceptable record of social orderliness. At most bus terminals in Nairobi and Addis Ababa, commuters stand in long queues awaiting their turn to get onto the bus. No one skips the queue to get favored seats ahead of fellow commuters. The system recognizes and prioritizes those who require assistance. The same orderliness is available and maintained in supermarkets, government offices, and airports. It is more strictly adopted in developed countries.

This orderliness is cultivated in citizens and becomes a way of life that people naturally adopt without government intervention. At traffic lights, the first driver stops, waiting for the light to turn green. The second driver pulls behind the first driver, and the third driver pulls behind the second, with the pedestrian line left clear for pedestrians to walk undisturbed. Traffic police and law-enforcement agencies are not always visible, but are available at short notice to maintain and restore order in case of a breach of orderliness. But the rule is that most citizens know and respect the order.

While some could assume that these signs of orderliness may be unintended habits, I am inclined to think otherwise. Orderliness begins with simple, unnoticed manners, such as respecting the service line, valuing the time of fellow citizens, and refraining from littering the streets. These trivial manners develop into the collective character of valued citizenship. One can see that ignoring these trivial manners develops into more destructive tendencies, such as siphoning the public coffers, accepting bribes, and selling the country's secrets and resources to foreigners.

The common denominator is being selfish, i.e., hyperbolic self-love. Selfishness prompts a driver to pull ahead of a fellow driver for an inherent belief that they are better or more deserving than the other. This is not a rule of thumb, as a driver having an emergency or carrying a sick person may justifiably want to get ahead of the queue, but these exceptions are rare. Selfishness prompts commuters to steal the position of their fellow commuter in the bus queue. The same selfishness pushes public officers to steal public money because they believe they deserve it more than their fellow citizens. On aggregate, individual behaviors add up to collective behavior, and the outcome is the country's regression, loss of respect, and underdevelopment.

Lack of orderliness is sometimes driven by inherent impatience or fear of losing something valuable. It is created from scarcity or the perception of it. It reflects the feeling that you won't get what you want without running or fighting. Simply put, it is a byproduct of the government's inability to provide comfort to citizens. Sudan has suffered from cyclical economic regression, leading to uncertainty about goods supply and service delivery, creating an environment where citizens fear what tomorrow holds. The same uncertainty about the future prompts suppliers to hoard commodities or increase prices; they can do so undisturbed, because of a lack of proper monitoring from the government.

What do you do if you are unsure that what you purchase today will be available tomorrow? Rational behavior implies buying copious quantities if one can afford it. If not, one may increase purchasing frequency to secure supply when stocks run dry. In both cases, you have created an artificial demand and contributed to increasing the price multiple times. This same logic applies equally to non-paid services. When people get anxious about the unknown, they secure themselves by overdemanding, overreacting, overeating, or becoming overdefensive.

One way this bad habit can be reversed is the advent of a national leader who builds historical consensus and calls for all Sudanese to look back on themselves and to generate a societal movement toward orderliness. These historic moments are sparse but possible. Al-Imam Al-Mahdi unified the country around a movement and effectively sowed the seeds of a Sudanese nation.[61] Prime Minister Hamdok had this historic moment to build a national drive toward citizenship, but his tenure was interrupted and ultimately collapsed. President Al-Bashir generated a similar consensus in his first days in office, but matters degenerated for reasons I refrain from mentioning in this book.[10]

The opportunity presented to the Sudanese under Prime Minister Hamdok was probably the kind that only comes once in a lifetime. It was an excellent occasion to break with a past characterized by spirals of vengeance. If the Sudanese had space for forgiveness—including forgiving the members of the National Congress Party (supporters of President Al-Bashir)—and called for an inclusive dialogue toward forming a national unity government, things would have been progressively different by now. The National Congress Party ruled for 30 years and built a solid financial and political dynasty that could not be undone in a few months. There could have been a more practical and winning way to reintegrate them into the new dispensation, while those proven corrupt could face the law in an orderly manner.

Socioeconomic Chronicles

- *Distorted Education System*

There has been a noticeable trend of commercialization of the education system in Sudan with the increased number of private schools, which parents perceive as more attractive than public schools. Parents who can send their children to private schools are perceived to be higher in status.

Government schools gradually deteriorated as teachers migrated to private schools for better pay. Those who could not afford private schools had to be content with keeping their children in government schools. This meant that, progressively, poverty was combined with low-quality education, which, in turn, only compounded poverty. Education is one of the most effective means to fight poverty. If you are poor and cannot educate your children, you die poor, and your children grow up and stay in poverty. It also means that the rich get richer because their children are better educated, ensuring a brighter future.

This inequality fuels social instability and conflicts in the long term. With limited options, the poor children may be recruited by militant groups, be content with low-quality subsistence labor, or flee the country to seek opportunities elsewhere. Being recruited by militant groups leads to radicalization or ending up in jail. Low-quality subsistence labor will rarely pull a person out of poverty. Fleeing the country without a reliable plan entails a considerable gamble with uncertain outcomes. In short, all these options are precarious and will likely lead to a bleak future.

■ *Undersupplied Social Infrastructure*

Investment in social infrastructure has been deficient in recent years. Hospitals exist in dire conditions, with inadequate equipment, prompting most Sudanese who can afford it to seek treatment abroad. Outbound and inbound flights from Egypt, Turkey, and Jordan are packed with elderly sick persons—accompanied by their close relatives—seeking treatment for ailments that should be easily treatable within the country, with reasonable investments.

A Sudanese friend told me that he took his sick mother to the UK and was admitted to a hospital in London, only to be treated by a senior Sudanese doctor who happened to be practicing there. Those doctors left the country to look for a better life. The Ministry of Health estimates that around 50 thousand Sudanese doctors live and work abroad. This is a sign of "brain drain" migration, but, more importantly, it means that those doctors who have been educated from the Sudanese taxpayers' money are now benefiting other nations.

The World Health Organization's Global Health Statistics 2022 report estimates there are 2.6 doctors per 10,000 people in Sudan, while the Sustainable Development Goals set a minimum of 44 doctors per 10,000 people. The doctors working abroad help the country through money transfers to their families. However, the core services for which they have been educated and trained no longer benefit the country. If more doctors educated in Sudan chose to remain there, Sudan could become one of the centers of excellence in medical treatment in Africa and beyond.

- *Destruction of Prime Institutions*

Over many years, Sudan built excellent aviation, shipping, railway, and seaport services. Sudan Airways used to be one of the few African carriers connecting Africa with Europe and East Asia. Sudan Shipping Lines was one of

Africa's most highly respected sea lines. Sudan Railways connected the country from north to south and east to west. At present, only fond memories are left of these prime institutions. Sudan Airways was founded in 1946, one year after Ethiopian Airlines.[62] Kenya Airways was founded in 1977,[63] and Rwandair in 2002.[64] Kenya Airways has 35 aircraft and a regional hub today, and Ethiopian Airlines has over 100 aircraft and a regional maintenance center.[65]

Rwandair is a different story. I was part of a team offered an assignment in 2007 to conduct a field appraisal for the acquisition of the first Bombardier CRJ-900 for Rwandair. I visited Kigali in the company of my good friend Moses Mwangi, who later became the chief finance officer of Rwandair. We completed the project and delivered the first Bombardier CRJ to Kigali in 2009. By the time I authored this book, Rwandair had 13 aircraft, including three Airbus A-330, six Boeing-737, two Bombardier CRJ-900, and two Dash 8-Q400. Meanwhile, Sudan Airways has three aircraft, two under lease. What went wrong?

There is no single answer to this question. Those seeking an answer should not target the technical and managerial personnel of the company. They are helpless. Instead, those seeking an answer should first address the multifaceted aspect of regression. I attempted to enumerate some of these aspects in the previous sections. I believe a sustainable answer should not be explored by witch-hunting but by courageous acknowledgment of the problem and journeying toward an honest and inclusive solution. Nations rise and fall as one unit. Therefore, finding a lasting answer should encompass this integrated approach to the problem rather than adopting a piecemeal solution.

Conclusion

An immediate question one may ask is, in what way do these elements relate to the war in Sudan? The answer is that war has direct and indirect triggers. The direct triggers are the visible causes, while the indirect triggers are supporting elements contributing to sustaining the fighting, aggravating its impacts, or hindering the efforts to stop the war.

For instance, the inability to accept each other, social deprivation, and politicization of civil services create an antagonizing environment and feeling of injustice, where a simple misunderstanding could be taken as a sufficient alibi to start the fighting.

Excessive musclism inclinations and the culture of pretentiousness generate an attitude that makes one perceive self-restraint and tolerance as cowardly.

A deformed education system and the destruction of social infrastructure increase unemployment and illiteracy, making unemployed persons easy targets for recruitment into illegal activities.

In the previous sections, I attempted to diagnose the root causes of Sudan's regression while its regional neighbors have made bold steps toward progress. Sudan's problem is a structural one and must be addressed accordingly. Based on the various social ailments and negative behavioral attributes observed and recounted in the previous sections, it should be clear that the war that erupted in Khartoum on April 15, 2023, was no more than the demolition of a building that has been deteriorating for decades. An ailing structure weakened by a progressive social tremor left untreated for a long time. This transformed the people into uncommitted citizens.

Over the years, people have been sedated by fallacious stereotypes about being peaceful citizens. There had never been such an awakening shock that prompted them to question those assumptions until the SAF and RSF collaboratively demolished the building. But what a demolition! One that seems to have wiped it out from the foundation upward. The question hitherto asked was not the shape and color of the condemned structure but whether a more solid and sustainable edifice could be erected to stand the test of time. More so, the question was whether the Sudanese could boldly divorce their emotions from the nostalgia of what has been lost and erect a nation-state that nurtures every inhabitant, irrespective of their skin color or religious inclinations.

I lived in Kenya for over 15 years and witnessed the 2007 and 2013 post-election violence. The violence was contained in a relatively brief time in both cases. Many factors seem to have contributed to the containment of the violence. First, the Kenyan police handled it with apparent professionalism. Second, religious leaders, both Christians and Muslims, were very vocal, preaching for peace and stability. Third, the political leaders came out forcefully with calls to order. This decision was difficult for some politicians who felt they were denied victory, but they rose to the moment and prioritized national interests over personal gains. Finally, whereas the nature of the conflict in Kenya is markedly different from Sudan's conflict in many respects, it is observable that the Kenyan middle class and enlightened citizens played a supporting role by promptly ensuring that government institutions continued to operate and provide for citizens. This contributed to sustaining civil service operations during the days of violence.

In contrast, Sudan's capital city, Khartoum, was not resilient enough to withstand the violence. The civil service promptly collapsed. The Sudan Certificate Examinations were skipped, representing a potentially irreversible break in the education chain. Barely a week after the fighting erupted, most international organizations and embassies packed and left the country swiftly when there was no clear roadmap for the end of the war.

One counterargument is the dissimilarity between the nature of the conflict in Kenya and Sudan, as the former was a political protest while the latter was a military conflict. True, but Kenyan protagonists reacted positively to the mediation efforts led by religious leaders and international partners.

In Sudan's case, the stubbornness was unmatched, as evidenced by the numerous failed mediation efforts. The conflict was taken as a zero-sum game by the Sudanese warring parties, while the parties to the Kenyan dispute believed a win-win situation could be achieved.

In the next chapter, I will discuss the transition challenges facing Sudan in consideration of similar historical challenges that South Sudan and Kenya have faced. The lessons learned from these two nations will form the basis for Sudan's roadmap to recovery.

Chapter Three

RETHINKING THE FRAGILITY CHRONICLE

Introduction

In this chapter, I will speak a word of caution. I discuss significant challenges facing post-conflict transition to recovery based on comparative assessment. I use the South Sudan case for comparison and supplement it with Kenya as a secondary case, based on several similarities between Sudan and Kenya, particularly concerning tribalism and social fluidity.

South Sudan offers critical lessons that urge caution toward the challenges that Sudan should mitigate in its quest to lay a foundation for lasting peace and stability. The southern country's sociopolitical history is intertwined with Sudan's, having seceded barely a decade ago. It has experienced internal peace and stability challenges since gaining independence, especially in the immediate years following independence. While it enjoyed relative stability since 2020, the peace in South Sudan remains fragile and volatile. Similar to the case of Sudan, the outbreak of civil war in South Sudan was due to a power struggle between two leaders in control of armed groups.[66] Last, given the currency of peace and conflict events in South Sudan, the experiences are one of the most contemporary and contextually relevant case studies to learn from.

The relevance of Kenya to my case is based on the significant challenges they face that speak to potential pitfalls for Sudan. Moreover, the demand for equity and justice remains a prominent topic of discussion at the national level and constitutes a key feature of political nonconformity that continues to grow. The challenges facing Sudan and similar contexts are enormous and many, but I summarize the most relevant ones since this book intends to provide immediate resources for urgent measures to achieve sustainable peace and stability in Sudan. These challenges include a lack of capacity, infrastructure deficiency, security threats, impunity, and resource constraints.

Lack of Legal Capacity

Lack of capacity is one of Sudan's most significant challenges in its quest for post-conflict transition. In South Sudan, this manifested in the shortage of legal professionals with competence and expertise in international humanitarian law and the transitional justice ecosystem. This inadequacy of skilled personnel posed a significant challenge to investigating and prosecuting culprits of atrocities committed during the conflict.[67] Lack of legal capacity undermined the institution of specialized courts and slowed justice delivery.

As citizens flee the country because of insecurity, human capital flight is inevitable.

The implication is that upon ceasefire, there will be inadequate local personnel capacity to process the numerous cases overflowing the justice system. In Sudan, for instance, the conflict destroyed the judicial infrastructure, including court buildings and administrative systems. The lack of functioning courts and appropriate facilities created obstacles in conducting fair and timely trials.

Rebuilding the judicial infrastructure requires significant time and resources, further delaying justice delivery and affecting public trust in the system.[68] Some cases from the Darfur conflict were elevated to the International Criminal Court (ICC) for prosecution, but again, the process faced momentous challenges, such as witness intimidation and deliberate withholding or destruction of evidence to sustain impunity.[69]

Sudan is also grappling with weak institutional frameworks to address the complex issues arising from the conflict.[40] This includes gaps in legislation, rules of procedure, and mechanisms for truth-seeking, reconciliation, and reparations of personal and property damages arising from the conflict. The absence of clear legal frameworks hinders Sudan's ability to hold those responsible for atrocities accountable and undermines efforts to achieve resilient peace and justice.[70]

Infrastructure Deficiency

Because war destroys infrastructure, available functioning infrastructure is often inadequate, making it difficult for civil war victims to access justice and participate in legal processes. Proper storage and archiving of case files are essential for the efficient functioning of the justice system.[71] Inadequate physical infrastructure can result in limited or inadequate storage space for case files, exhibits, and other legal documents. This can lead to difficulty locating and retrieving information, which increases the chance of errors, delays, or loss of critical evidence.[71]

The availability of appropriate transport and detention facilities is vital. Inadequate physical infrastructure and transportation systems—including damaged roads, insufficient vehicles, or lack of secure prisoner transport—can hinder the timely transfer of detainees to and from court hearings. South Sudan's post-conflict justice system has faced these challenges, resulting in disorganized records and difficulty locating and retrieving information when needed.[72]

Physical infrastructure plays a crucial role in ensuring the security and safety of all stakeholders involved in the justice process. Inadequate infrastructure can compromise the safety of judges, lawyers, witnesses, and other personnel working within the justice system.[73] Insufficient security measures—such as a lack of secure entrances, screening facilities, or surveillance systems—can increase vulnerability to threats, attacks, or interference, impacting the integrity and independence of the justice process. The lack of ramps, elevators, or specialized facilities can impede physical access and create barriers, especially for vulnerable groups and those disabled due to war.[73]

Marginalized groups, including ethnic or religious minorities, women, persons with disabilities, and IDPs, may face challenges accessing justice institutions. Factors such as geographical remoteness, lack of transportation, language barriers, or cultural biases can hinder their physical presence at courts, police stations, or legal aid offices. Limited access prevents marginalized groups from seeking justice, reporting crimes, or participating effectively in legal processes.[74]

War victims often have limited knowledge about their rights and available remedies. This lack of legal awareness prevents them from accessing justice effectively. The absence of affordable and culturally sensitive legal representation can marginalize these groups, as they may struggle to navigate complex legal systems, may not understand their legal rights, and present their cases inadequately. In addition, poverty, illiteracy, and dependency on informal economies prevent them from accessing legal services, paying legal fees, or attending court proceedings. This is because they must balance meeting their survival needs and seeking justice.[75] The dwellers of IDP camps in Darfur live on less than a dollar a day and depend on food distributed by non-governmental organizations. The IDPs have limited income-generating options because of a lack of education. Therefore, they have neither the financial resources nor the technical knowledge to seek justice, which is not even a priority for someone struggling to keep their family alive.

Victims of sexual abuse and other atrocities are often underrepresented in decision-making processes related to post-conflict justice and legal reforms. Their voices and perspectives may not be adequately heard or considered, leading to the exclusion of their specific needs and concerns in policy development and implementation. In most cases, victims of rape often shy away from presenting their cases for fear of stigma.

In Sudan, rape is almost equivalent to a death sentence because of the long-term and irreparable stigma that goes beyond the victim to deliver damaging emotional and social impact on the entire family. This lack of representation can perpetuate systemic inequalities and hinder the creation of inclusive and responsive justice systems. This becomes a recipe for future civil unrest, especially when discrimination and feelings of marginalization continue.[76]

Security Threats

One consequence of the lack of capacity is security threats posed by armed groups and militias. These are a common theme in post-conflict societies and pose a significant challenge to justice delivery in different ways.[77] This is due to armed groups' continued existence and operation beyond the ceasefire. The presence of such armed groups creates an intimidating environment that undermines the safety and security of victims, witnesses, judicial personnel, and all those who are parties to the justice process.

Harassment and aggression targeting seekers of justice discourage people from coming forward and supporting the work of authorities or offering crucial testimonies, thus inhibiting the advancement of investigations and trials. For example, armed groups continued to operate following the ceasefire in Darfur. Consequently, individuals afraid of reprisals and concerned about the lack of security were reluctant to come forward or cooperate with the authorities, making it difficult for justice to be served.

War also creates fertile ground for small arms proliferation. Pistols, AK-47 rifles, and hand grenades are displayed and sold at open-air markets in conflict zones. Not only that, but they are also made affordable to most people.[67] This makes tracing and retrieving weapons difficult when peace finally prevails.

Strong incentives must be put in place to encourage civilians to hand over arms in their possession voluntarily. Sudan tried using a carrot-and-stick policy to collect arms in Darfur, without success. This time, I believe the international community should be involved in a wide-scale program that should benefit from donor funding and borrow from the experiences of Mozambique, Liberia, and Sierra Leone, among others.

Armed groups and militias also often control certain territories or communities, holding undue influence and power over the local justice system. As a result, they may impose their justice mechanisms or obstruct the functioning of official post-conflict justice institutions. This parallel justice system frequently lacks fairness, impartiality, and adherence to human rights standards, leading to a lack of trust in the formal justice process and undermining the credibility and effectiveness of the post-conflict justice ecosystem.[78]

Some armed groups and militias in Sudan exerted control over certain Darfur territories, allowing them to influence and manipulate local justice systems. Such militias often seek to cushion any members implicated in atrocities during the conflict by using various tactics to shield perpetrators from accountability, such as hiding them, providing false alibis, or obstructing access to evidence. This protection can impede the investigation and prosecution of those responsible for human rights abuses.[78]

Another challenge is that armed groups and militias often operate in remote or inaccessible areas, frustrating the ability of justice institutions to investigate. Their presence may restrict the movement of judicial personnel and hinder the collection of evidence, witness testimonies, and documentary proof. Armed groups often refuse to cooperate with or obstruct the work of justice institutions, denying access to crucial information and hindering the pursuit of justice.[78] This was the case in Darfur, where the pursuit of justice became severely hampered and ultimately escalated the conflict. Post-conflict societies often face the challenge of reintegrating former combatants from armed groups and militias into society.[79]

Balancing the need for justice and accountability with the imperative of facilitating their reintegration is a complex task. Designing and implementing effective reintegration programs that address the reasons for their involvement in armed groups while ensuring accountability for crimes committed can be challenging. Sudan faced this challenge after the Darfur conflict.

Impunity and Lack of Trust

Impunity is the failure to bring perpetrators of injustice to book. When those who control instruments of power undermine the rule of law, public trust is eroded, and people lose confidence in any associated justice system.[80] When perpetrators of atrocities go scot-free, it signals that one can commit a crime and get away with it. This can perpetuate a cycle of vengeance-driven atrocities and hamper the process of reconciliation and healing.

Kenya faced challenges in addressing impunity for perpetrators of injustices, particularly during political violence, such as the post-election violence in 2007–2008.[81] The lack of accountability and effective prosecution of those responsible for crimes has perpetuated a culture of impunity.

A study examining the example of Kenya's Truth, Justice, and Reconciliation Commission (TJRC) noted that despite the commission not being able to fully achieve its objective of overcoming numerous obstacles to establish the groundwork for reconciliation, it served as a solace for the victims to finally see a genuine effort toward acknowledging the injustices committed against them.[82] Hence, an attempt like the Kenyan TJRC is an indispensable element of justice in post-conflict situations.

Another study by Amnesty International revealed a sense of disillusionment and despair among individuals seeking recovery from the social, economic, and psychological consequences of the Kenyan post-election violence.[83] A similar narrative is echoed in a study that analyzed the efforts of Kenya's TJRC and discovered that since the country's independence, victims of violence and human rights abuses in Kenya have largely been denied justice.[84]

The justice system is often distrusted in post-conflict settings because of biased practices and corruption. The perception of an unfair or ineffective justice system creates disillusionment among the affected population. This lack of trust can lead to underreporting of crimes, reluctance to engage with justice mechanisms, and a general belief that seeking justice is a waste of time and effort. It poses a significant obstacle to the delivery of post-conflict justice and impedes the establishment of sustainable peace.

Impunity and lack of trust can contribute to witnesses' reluctance to come forward and provide testimonies.

Distrust of authorities and concerns for personal safety can discourage witnesses from participating in investigations or testifying in court, therefore hampering the gathering of crucial evidence for effective prosecution and impeding the pursuit of justice. This was evident in the case of Darfur, where fear of reprisal inhibited the course of justice as victims and witnesses were reluctant to come forward, potentially leading to the failure of local justice mechanisms to prosecute pending cases.

In many post-conflict societies, witnesses lack confidence in the ability of the justice system to protect them. They often believe that coming forward will not result in meaningful justice. Without a credible and effective justice system, victims and affected communities may struggle to find closure, reconcile with their past, and rebuild trust within their societies. Justice mechanisms that fail to address the principal drivers of conflicts and provide redress for victims perpetuate cycles of violence and can impede long-term stability and reconciliation efforts.[85]

Resource Constraints

Post-conflict societies often face significant financial constraints as they strive to rebuild and recover from the aftermath of conflict. The allocation of limited resources becomes complex, with numerous sectors vying for funding, including healthcare, education, infrastructure, and economic development. In this context, allocating sufficient resources to the justice sector becomes challenging, as it competes with other pressing needs and demands.

For instance, Sudan faces significant financial constraints as it rebuilds and recovers from years of conflict.[86] The limited financial resources for justice delivery deprive the establishment of robust post-conflict justice mechanisms and capacity-building efforts.[87] While Sudan may enjoy vast resources and assets, the most critical resources needed for post-conflict reconstruction have already been damaged by the civil war, which strains available resources.

Evidence from South Sudan indicates that the country grappled with ongoing humanitarian crises, including food insecurity, displacement, and healthcare challenges.[88] Addressing these urgent humanitarian needs takes precedence in resource allocation, as the immediate survival and wellbeing of the population are paramount.

Post-conflict Sudan must rebuild physical infrastructure, such as roads, schools, hospitals, and water supply systems, which are essential for the wellbeing and functioning of the country. The need to prioritize essential services and infrastructure development may result in limited resources for strengthening the justice system, impeding the effective delivery of post-conflict justice. Furthermore, addressing poverty and unemployment and promoting socioeconomic development are crucial for post-conflict societies to achieve stability and prevent future conflicts.

Conclusion

In this chapter, I have drawn attention to the five significant challenges likely to confront post-conflict justice delivery in Sudan. Underlying the challenges are competing resource allocation priorities requiring a comprehensive and coordinated approach.

In this book, I argue that the first step to addressing the Sudanese problem is to revisit the nation's core identity and ask a fundamental question of who the Sudanese really are. The next chapter begins the second section of the book, "Resolving the Puzzles," where I critically revisit some fundamental issues of national identity and relate them to similar experiences from select African nations.

The discussion in this section forms the foundation for recovery by breaking the historical legacies that, in some ways, may have contributed to initiating, proliferating, and prolonging the conflicts, leading to wars, destruction, and famine.

Hence, I reserve the next chapter to discuss some historical narratives that were hitherto held as absolute truisms, where I argue that the first step to finding a better version of Sudan begins with admitting that the previous version did not work. Accordingly, I will discuss the quest for a unifying national identity to achieve a nationwide movement for peace, mutual acceptance, and the rule of law.

Chapter Four

RESOLVING THE NATIONAL IDENTITY PUZZLE

Introduction

The word "Sudanism" was first hinted at in a speech by the late John Garang in 1995 while referring to Arabo-Islamism as a culture the north tries to impose on the Afro-Christian south.[89] Sudanism was later referred to in an article by Roba Gibia in 2005. Gibia wrote: "Why Arabism and Islam and why not Sudanism, if one may ask?"[90] Sudanism represents a search for identity and echoes transitional moments in other nations' histories. These transitions are typically characterized by moments of reckoning when leaders rose to chart a path for nations divided along ethnic or tribal lines.

I define Sudanism thus: "Sudanism is a unique identity that transcends cultural, ethnic, and religious boundaries to premise an individual's rights and obligations on the sole foundation of being Sudanese." In that respect, Sudanism bears the traits of a culturally diverse, religiously tolerant, and emotionally peaceful person. Various African nations experienced these precarious transitional moments and produced momentous leaders who managed to build consensus around principles of nationhood. Sudanism thus echoes the Ujamaa philosophy in Tanzania, the Harambee philosophy in Kenya, and the Ubuntu philosophy in Rwanda and South Africa, to name just a few.

Tanzania's Ujamaa

Historically known as "Tanganyika," Tanzania was another African nation that suffered a history of ethnic and tribal divides.[91] In 1962, Mwalimu Julius Kambarage Nyerere became the first national president of Tanzania one year after they gained independence. The country went through turmoil and internal war over the unification of Tanganyika and Zanzibar, where the name "Tanzania" originated. Mwalimu Nyerere took bold steps toward nation-building by merging his party, Tanganyika African National Union (TANU), with Zanzibar's ruling party, the Afro-Shirazi Party (ASP).[91] Nyerere also introduced a Pan-African Socialism philosophy, fondly known among Tanzanians as "*Ujamaa*," which means "extended family or familyhood."

Ujamaa contributed to building the foundations of a nation-state in Tanzania by fostering the values of solidarity, productivity, and the spirit of nationalism.[92] Ujamaa made it undesirable for Tanzanians to identify themselves along tribal and ethnic divides. Under the Ujamaa spirit, the government adopted positive discrimination by implementing production and distribution policies that favored rural Tanzania and vulnerable groups.[92] Today, Tanzania is one of the most peaceful countries in Africa, with tested democracy, rule of law, and good citizenship behavior.

Her Excellency Samia Suluhu was sworn in as Tanzania's President on March 19, 2021, following the death of President John Pombe Magufuli.[93] I visited Dar-es-Salaam several times, and every time I was there, I could not help but marvel at the Tanzanians. What caught my attention the most were the Christian ladies dressed in Muslim attire. At times, you could not tell the ethnic origin of a Tanzanian from their name. This signifies that Tanzanians have long since moved on to become truly one nation.

Kenya's Harambee

In Kenya, "*Harambee*" is a sacred word that denotes "pulling all together." Harambee connotes a sense of togetherness, solidarity, and shared destiny.[94] During my first months of relocation to Nairobi as an international staff member, Kenyan colleagues helped me quickly settle. I still remember a Kenyan friend driving me around to look for apartments, visiting schools to enroll my children, and even sampling eateries and supermarkets.

I came to know Harambee in my first days in Nairobi when friends came together to collect money for the burial and funeral of the mother of one of our drivers. Later, I learned that Harambee is deeper and more expanded in the spirits of Kenyans than just financial contributions for social occasions. The Kenyan National Football team is called the Harambee Stars. The Kenyan National Anthem, "*Ee Mungu Nguvu Yetu*," solidifies the Harambee principles.

[95] Although Kenya has historically suffered divisions along tribal lines, the country quickly weathered conflicts and avoided degenerating into full-blown civil war through leaders' commitment to mediation, dialogue, and a spirit of reconciliation and compromise.

Rwanda's Ubuntu

Rwanda hit the rock bottom of national chaos during the 1994 genocide. This had built up for decades and exploded in 1994 when nearly a million Hutus and moderate Tutsis were raped, slaughtered, or burned alive from April 7th to July 15th in what is commonly known as the *100-day massacre*.[96] I met an elderly Rwandan citizen in Kigali in 2007 and asked him about the 1994 genocide. He said, "You know, I don't want to speak about it again. We became like sharks. We ate each other alive."

Rwanda has since moved on and built a nation-state where bearers of the citizenship document only identify themselves as "*a Rwandan.*" This unification of cause and allegiance to the flag was partly made possible by the advent of visionary leadership that unified the Rwandans around a national identity, "*Ubuntu.*"[97]

Ubuntu is proudly used in Rwanda to connote solidarity, interconnectedness, and interdependence of individuals within the community. Ubuntu encompasses empathy, compassion, and mutual respect. Ubuntu was the elixir that healed the wounds, tamed the emotions, and reconciled the differences, creating a proud Rwandan identity. Ubuntu meant hard work, pride in citizenship, and individual vision. Ubuntu would not have been possible without practical steps taken by leaders and communities to heal the wounds of the war.

South Africa's Ubuntu

South Africans have their own version of Ubuntu.[98] The word *"Ubuntu"* technically has comparable definitions in Rwanda and South Africa, but the colors and flavors differ in how it is experienced.[99] This is the beauty of culture. Ubuntu was already popular in South Africa, but the Late Archbishop Reverend Desmond Tutu flavored it with a taste of spiritual purity and religious faith to salvage his nation. [100] The Archbishop Reverend describes Ubuntu as "the essence of being human."[101]

The Rwandan flavor of "Ubuntu" is "live with each other and for each other." South African Ubuntu is flavored with the core value of humanity to treat the social malady of human disparagement, as evidenced in how black South Africans were treated in apartheid.[101] Rwandan Ubuntu was flavored by the core value of togetherness to treat the social malady of capital exclusion, i.e., denying a fellow citizen the right to life, as demonstrated in the genocide.[102]

The common denominator in South African and Rwandan versions of Ubuntu is upholding the core values of humanity. Ubuntu was a rallying cry that shook the two great nations to awaken and prompted them to look back onto themselves in a moment of reckoning as if everyone cried with full throat: "We are better, and we deserve better." However, this is only possible when a nation is blessed with gifted leaders.[103]

Sudanism as an Inspirer of National Identity

Like Tanzania's Ujamaa, Kenyan's Harambee, and Rwanda's and South Africa's Ubuntu, Sudan can grow Sudanism into a rallying call to unite the nation around a national identity. This does not mean that "Sudanism" must be strictly adopted. Other words or phrases can be suggested. The bottom line is that the word should represent the entirety of Sudan, be easy to pronounce and understand, and connote Sudan's desired cultural identity.

Sudan has never successfully built a national identity with which every Sudanese can identify. This is evidenced by the country's lack of a stable constitution since independence, persistent failure to sustain power alternation through democratic practice, and inability to find a lasting solution to the recurrence of resistance movements. Through Sudanism, the Sudanese should endeavor to relinquish allegiance to tribal domes and cliquish exclusivity in favor of "Sudan."

In a nutshell, Ubuntu is derived from Kinyarwanda, the national language of Rwanda.[97] Ujamaa and Harambee are derived from Kiswahili, the national languages of Tanzania and Kenya.[91] In Sudan's case, although Arabic is a widely spoken language, diversity is such that other non-Arab ethnic groups have their own languages and cultures, which they desire to promote side by side with Arabic cultures. Likewise, political Islam did not unify the country but led to the disintegration of the south. Therefore, insistence on the Arabo-Islamic culture may lead to further disintegration of areas such as the Blue Nile, Nuba Mountains, Darfur, eastern Sudan, and the Nubians in the north.

Therefore, I submit that only Sudanism can unify Sudan. Sudanism is odorless, only scented in the people's collective solidarity; Sudanism is colorless, only colored by the cultural rainbow of the nation; Sudanism is shapeless, only shaped by the people's willingness and readiness to accept one another. To avoid doubt or confusion, Sudanism is not a word or term but a way of life, a culture, and an identity. As such, Sudanism tolerates cultural diversity and fosters belonging, regardless of language, faith, or skin color.

The National Anthem of Sudan is entitled, "We Are the Army of God and the Army of Our Land." The anthem was adopted and sung on Independence Day, January 1, 1956. [104] The original version of the anthem is written in Arabic. I searched online and found more than five versions of the translation into English, but in my view, this one is the most accurate translation:

> We are the army of God and of our land,
> We shall never fail when called to sacrifice.
> Whether braving death, hardship, or pain,
> We give our lives as a price for glory.
> May this Our land, Sudan, live long,
> Showing all nations the way.
> Sons of the Sudan, summoned now to serve,
> Shoulder the task of preserving our country.[104]

This national anthem was relevant at the time it was written to hail the sacrifices of the Sudanese who struggled to achieve independence. But is it still relevant now? A national anthem summarizes a nation's pride, what differentiates it from other nations, and what the country can contribute to making the world better. It also expresses a nation's unity and solidarity without ignoring diversity.

The national anthem seems to have tilted heavily toward a nation's sacrifice to repel or defeat the enemies of the land. While this is a noble cause, the anthem could have incorporated other fundamental aspects, such as promoting productivity, national unity, and progress. I submit that a forward-looking Sudan should consider proposing an amendment to the national anthem to incorporate these aspects. If the anthem was adopted from a longer text, it may be worthwhile to enrich it with new lyrics from the main text or add new lyrics altogether.

Rewriting or amending the national anthem constitutes one aspect of the fundamental changes that should be introduced to solidify the principle of Sudanism. While some may consider this a wild notion, parting with an adverse historical legacy requires revolutionary thinking. The old mindset will only reproduce failure after failure. It is more than enough that the Sudanese failed to build a nation they will be proud of after 67 years of trial and error. Now, they must try something else.

Conclusion

With all the elements of a great country—rich history, excellent geographic location, rich resource base, and populous neighborhoods—Sudan failed to capitalize on this potential to build a resilient economy and coherent nation-state. The country has been on a regressive trajectory with no clear path to the future. A structural approach was adopted in the previous chapters to diagnose the origins of the problem by looking beyond the surface to unearth the sociocultural as well as economic and political aspects.

Sudan's ideal treatment must not neglect those finer elements of the problem. In the next chapter, I will discuss some case studies of recovery roadmaps from selected African countries that share similarities with Sudan's case. These include Rwanda, Angola, Sierra Leone, Mozambique, and South Africa.

Chapter Five

RESOLVING THE RECOVERY GRIDLOCK PUZZLE

Introduction

Like most African countries that transitioned from civil war and charted a steady recovery path, Sudan cannot expect to be the exception to the rule of chaos. Several potential routes and options for recovery and development in Sudan can be identified based on the experiences of other hitherto fragile or transitioned countries, notably Rwanda, Angola, Sierra Leone, Mozambique, and South Africa.

Each of these countries inherited a legacy of exclusion or repression and faced enormous challenges in constructing foundations for a nation-state.[105] Each country also experienced human rights violations and institutionalized impunity. In each of these countries, victims and their allies in civil society persisted in their demands for truth, justice, and reparations. That persistence—combined with alliance-building with local civil society organizations, international human rights groups and institutions, and actors in key state institutions—became the driving force in charting a path to recovery.[80]

In this chapter, I discuss the principles of recovery in Sudan's war through a comparative lens based on similar examples within the African context. I focus on how these countries broke from the zero-sum civil war game to chart a path toward lasting peace. Specifically, I draw out lessons that Sudan can learn from the experiences of these countries on the more critical matters of transitional justice, strengthening of institutions of governance, and economic recovery and development. I discuss how ceasefire and transitional justice were achieved in Mozambique. I also discuss the practical cases from Angola's post-conflict institutional reforms and Sierra Leone's recovery path. I further discuss two transitional justice and social peace cases, notably the South African Truth and Reconciliation Commission of the Late Archbishop Reverend Desmond Tutu and the *Gacaca* Courts in Rwanda.

Several commonalities are evident between Sudan, Mozambique, South Africa, Rwanda, Angola, and Sierra Leone. All five cases are in Africa; all went through social strife and political turmoil and transitioned to social justice through protracted and intermediated negotiation processes. Based on this comparative assessment, I argue that peace is only attainable through a participatory approach that brings together all parties and builds social integration using a bottom-up approach.

Rwanda Post-Genocide Transformation

The Rwanda genocide (April–July 1994) was a horrific event characterized by ethnic violence, profiling, and targeted extermination.[106] While the genocide took place many years after the country attained independence, the significance of Rwanda's case to Sudan lies in the fact that the genocide had roots back in the colonial era. Recall that the seeds of discord in present-day Sudan were sown in the colonial period. To rule Rwanda undisturbed, the occupiers sowed ethnic divisions between the Hutus and the Tutsis. One ethnic group, which primarily benefited from social and political changes, ascended to power and started discriminating against the other ethnic group.[107]

The next few decades that followed in Rwanda were characterized by ethnic tensions that escalated into waves of violence and, sometimes, massacres.[108] This peaked with full-blown genocide in 1994.[109] While peace talks began in 1993, culminating in the Arusha Agreement on power-sharing between the government and the Rwandan Patriotic Front (RPF), it was not until the government of Rwanda began implementing policies aimed at fostering unity and healing that the country began its break-away from the yoke of civil war to a long and winding path toward peace and stability.[96]

Central to this was promoting national identity over ethnic divisions. A series of grassroots efforts were initiated to foster dialogue, understanding, and empathy between different ethnic groups, emphasizing the shared Rwandan identity.[96] This was achieved by deliberately moving away from divisive ethnic profiling. Instead, the government emphasized common values, history, and aspirations for the future.

Rwanda also promoted social stability by becoming intentional in addressing inequality. President Kagame emphasized the importance of inclusivity, dialogue, and a long-term vision for the country. This underscores the concept of Sudanism, which must immediately become a rallying call loudly evident in the words and deeds of Sudanese, from the rulers to the populace.

While Rwanda's sociocultural context may have a certain uniqueness, Sudan can learn something from the successes of the *Gacaca* courts and adapt what worked for Rwanda to the Sudanese scene. These reparation initiatives pushed the perpetrators to recognize wrongs committed, as well as the pain and suffering of survivors. Survivors acknowledged the remorse among perpetrators, their humanity, and the poverty of their communities. This has seen the country heal and sustain durable peace that is frequently elusive in many post-conflict countries.[110] Reparation is thus hailed as the transitional justice mechanism with the most significant potential for socioeconomic impact in post-conflict countries.[80]

The *Gacaca* courts were designed to involve the local communities directly in the justice process.[111] These were community-based tribunals designed to try lower-level perpetrators of the genocide. Local communities played a central role in the operation of the courts, including the selection of judges and the resolution of cases.[112] The hearings took place in the communities where the injustices and human rights abuses occurred, allowing community members to participate as witnesses, judges, and observers.[102]

They allowed survivors to share their experiences, confront the perpetrators, and seek justice. Victims were encouraged to participate and present their testimonies, ensuring their voices were heard.[113]

The courts also empowered survivors to seek reparations and compensation for their losses. The courts aimed to bring justice to the victims and promote reconciliation by encouraging truth-telling, repentance, and forgiveness at the community level. They involved ordinary citizens serving as judges elected by their communities. The judges were chosen for their integrity and knowledge of the community members involved in the cases.

The courts facilitated identifying and returning stolen property to its rightful owners through a participatory approach involving community members.[114] The *Gacaca* process emphasized truth-telling and encouraged perpetrators to confess their crimes. Confessions were seen as a pathway to forgiveness and reconciliation. Perpetrators who confessed and showed remorse were often given reduced sentences.[115]

The *Gacaca* courts were firmly rooted in the Rwandan culture and traditional justice systems.[114] They, therefore, recognized the specific context of Rwandan society and its cultural norms. They incorporated traditional practices and structures, such as community mediators, emphasizing reconciliation and communal healing.[116] They drew on the *Gacaca* tradition of community dispute resolution, adapting it to deal with genocide-related crimes.[96] This approach provides crucial lessons for Sudan to break from the chain of repeated internal conflict.[102]

This context-sensitive approach recognized the importance of adapting justice mechanisms to fit the local context. In addition to adjudicating cases, the courts aimed to promote truth-telling, accountability, and reconciliation. This comprehensive approach addressed the roots of the genocide and fostered healing within communities.

Gacaca courts were thus part of a long-term transitional justice process in Rwanda. They were one of broader efforts that included educational programs, memorialization initiatives, and community-based reconciliation processes. The goal was to promote lasting peace, reconciliation, and the prevention of future conflicts by addressing the deep-seated divisions within Rwandan society.

As the Rwanda case has demonstrated, retributive justice occupies the most prominent space in transitional justice success, with measures such as trials and tribunals executed in line with criminal or public law. The predominant focus of judicial prosecution is to combat impunity, condemn or probe perpetrators, and establish or reform security. However, rehabilitation is also a standard measure Sudan can apply to deal with the past. Retributive justice can be considered an enabler of restorative justice because it prepares the ground for perpetrators to testify in front of commissions of inquiries, such as truth commissions, without the fear of retribution outside the justice system.

The *Gacaca* court system is a bottom-up approach to transitional justice. It encompasses guiding principles that emphasize the empowerment of individuals and communities, promote inclusivity, and address systemic injustices from the grassroots level. This model prioritizes the involvement of people and communities affected by injustices. It values the diversity of identities, experiences, and perspectives within society. It recognizes that justice-related challenges and solutions are context-specific. It fosters stakeholder collaboration based on the belief that collective action is often more potent than individual efforts. It underscores the need for long-term commitment to transition. It holds individuals and institutions accountable for decisions and actions.

The *Gacaca* courts system is premised on six principles: participation, ownership, victim-centrism, context sensitivity, exhaustiveness, and sustainability. The principles vary in relevance depending on the time elapsed since the conflict. For these principles to be sustainable eventually, there is a need to address the context of inequality that makes some members of society more vulnerable to violence. This has implications for policy reforms as part of the broader transitional justice mechanisms for Sudan.

In my view, Rwanda's *Gacaca* courts provide a classic example from which Sudan can learn, owing to the similarity of the two cultures. Rwandans and Sudanese lend strong allegiance to traditional and tribal systems, and both countries underwent history-long conflicts fueled by a perceived sentiment of marginalization.

The failure to adopt robust transitional justice policies that ensure integral reparations for victims—truth, justice, economic and symbolic reparations, and guarantees of non-repetition—weakens citizens' trust in government, undermines the consolidation of the rule of law, and makes national reconciliation an elusive goal. The weak implementation of transitional justice covers pro-impunity agents seeking to retain power and preserve their privilege, therefore undermining the rule of law and threatening instability.

Enforcement inadequacies, state interference, and limited local ownership hinder their effectiveness. Sudan must thus put effective implementation and deterrence measures in place.

Sudan can also take measures to guarantee non-repetition, which entails making the reforms necessary to protect human rights. Guarantees of non-repetition include measures that are overly broad in scope. The purpose goes beyond the reparation of victims to prevent future violations and protect communities from the horrors of violence. They are structural, and their effectiveness will be assessed in the long run. This materializes in measures such as ensuring the implementation of due process standards and impartiality in proceedings, strengthening the judiciary's independence, protecting legal, medical, and media professionals and human rights defenders, and reforming law where necessary.

Three lessons can be learned from the *Gacaca* courts that apply to Sudan. First, Sudan will only outgrow its vicious cycle of conflict when the affected communities are given a voice and actively participate in serving justice. Second, the participatory approach to justice will constitute a nucleus for a broad-based democratic exercise, considering that four generations of Sudanese have never had a chance to experience democratic practice. Third, the *Gacaca* courts will promote satisfactory justice delivery to bring lasting peace to Sudan.

Angola's Governance and Institutional Reforms

Angola has experienced several wars and conflicts throughout its history. The most notable and protracted conflict is the Angolan Civil War, which lasted from 1975 to 2002.[117]

The war began after the country gained independence. It broke out as a tug-of-war between the People's/Popular Movement for the Liberation of Angola (*Movimento Popular de Libertação de Angola*, or MPLA), led by Agostinho Neto, and the National Union for Total Independence of Angola (*União Nacional para a Independência Total de Angola*, or UNITA), led by Jonas Savimbi. The war had devastating consequences for Angola. It resulted in a widespread conflict characterized by intense fighting, including battles to capture or recapture key cities and control natural resources.[118]

The civil war ended when international mediators brokered a peace agreement between the two warring parties. The ensuing ceasefire agreement outlined a process for political reconciliation, which saw the incorporation of UNITA into the Angolan government.

UNITA's armed forces were to be incorporated into the Angolan Armed Forces (*Forças Armadas Angolanas*, or FAA), and the MPLA committed to integrating UNITA soldiers into the FAA's ranks.[119] Strengthened institutions increase the legitimacy and credibility of the process. Commitment to the transition in Angola entailed the disarmament, demobilization, rehabilitation, and reintegration (DDRR) of ex-combatants from the MPLA and UNITA forces.[118]

Disarming and demobilizing former fighters helped to reduce the risk of renewed conflict and fostered a sense of security among the population.[120] It took the mutual commitment of warring parties to de-escalate tensions by remaining faithful to the peace agreement. This shouldn't be elusive for Sudan, as the narratives are more or less identical.

The agreement also outlined the framework for holding elections, with UNITA participating as a political party. It provided for the demilitarization of politics and the estab-lishment of a democratic system. Following the bloodless uprising in Sudan, which deposed Al-Bashir as president, the Sudanese had begun a similar process, which could have seen the country sustain peace had it not been inter-rupted midway.

The reconciliation of the government and UNITA reb-els was crucial for establishing a stable and inclusive political environment.[121] Initiatives focused on promoting dialogue, trust-building, and national unity were prioritized. This involved incorporating former UNITA members into the political process, encouraging their participation in gover-nance, and addressing grievances peacefully. The fact that this was successful in Angola means that Sudan can achieve comparable results by strengthening governing institutions.

A key aspect of strengthening governing institutions is the establishment of electoral processes and democratic institutions. Establishing transparent and credible electoral processes was vital for democratic governance in Angola. [122] The development of electoral laws, the creation of in-dependent electoral commissions, and the organization of free and fair elections were critical priorities. These efforts aimed to promote democratic governance, ensure political representation, and foster a culture of participatory politics. [122] It took sacrificial leadership from both sides in Angola to maintain this path of post-conflict reconstruction. Sudan can take this path, too, if the spirit of Sudanism takes over.

Another crucial factor behind Angola's success was the development of comprehensive electoral laws that provided a legal framework for conducting elections. This involved drafting and enacting legislation that addressed electoral procedures, voter registration, campaign financing, political party regulations, and dispute resolution mechanisms. The laws ensured transparency, fairness, and credibility in the electoral process.[122] On this front, establishing independent electoral commissions was necessary for overseeing and administering elections. These commissions comprised impartial and non-partisan members responsible for managing various aspects of the electoral process, including voter registration, candidate nomination, ballot preparation, vote counting, and result announcement. Their independence and credibility were vital in building public trust in the electoral system in Angola. Sudan can benchmark against Angola and other countries with more mature democracies.

Angola established independent anti-corruption bodies. These institutions were mandated to investigate and prosecute corruption cases, enhance public administration transparency, and promote integrity in the public and private sectors. Strengthening anti-corruption agencies involves providing adequate resources, training, and legal powers to perform their duties effectively. These bodies contribute to checks and balances on potential abuse of office, and their effectiveness is hinged on political goodwill that must come from the people who control instruments of power. Sudan can learn from the Angola case study and its more stable neighbors.

Angola enhanced its civil service and public administration's capacity, professionalism, and efficiency. This involved revising human resource management practices, implementing merit-based recruitment and promotion systems, providing training and development opportunities for public servants, and establishing mechanisms for performance evaluation. Strengthening civil service aims to improve service delivery, professionalism, and public trust in government institutions. This is an antidote to the culture of cronyism, favoritism, nepotism, and discrimination in the distribution of employment opportunities. Eliminating these vices and pursuing professionalism in public service will go a long way toward enhancing the legitimacy of the ruling government and setting a firm foundation for lasting peace in Sudan.

Sierra Leone's Post-Conflict Recovery

Sierra Leone experienced a brutal civil war from 1991 to 2002, causing widespread devastation and economic collapse.[123] At the center of the civil war was the quest to control the country's abundant natural resources, especially diamonds, which benefited only a few elites at the expense of a significant share of the population languishing in poverty.[124] The country's ruler-ship was characterized by authoritarianism, high corruption, and mismanagement of resources. Consequently, a large mass of the population was disillusioned. This was a recipe for civil conflict that stoked a rebellion by a group known as the Revolutionary United Front (RUF), led by Foday Sankoh. In the decade between 1991 and 2002, the country was embroiled in a senseless civil war that halted Sierra Leone's economy.

The next decade began on the right foot for Sierra Leone with a momentary ceasefire.[123] Although the ceasefire did not last long, victory over RUF was only won when a peace agreement was signed between the government and RUF. The signing of the peace agreement marked the beginning of a determined journey toward rebuilding the country and its economy. Consequently, the country implemented economic reforms, attracted foreign investments, and focused on mining, agriculture, and tourism. These reforms aimed to improve governance, enhance transparency, and promote fiscal discipline. While challenges remain, Sierra Leone has shown resilience and achieved notable economic progress. Sudan can emulate this intentionality when it turns away its focus from *who* should govern the country to *how* it should be governed.

Sierra Leone has actively sought foreign investments to boost economic growth. The government engaged in investment promotion campaigns and participated in international conferences and forums to showcase opportunities in the country.[125] Special economic zones and investment incentives attracted foreign businesses. The government also engaged in public-private partnerships to encourage investments in critical infrastructure development and energy sectors.[126]

Like Sierra Leone, Sudan enjoys abundant resources that it can leverage to attract foreign investment through various economic incentives and public-private partnerships. A solid foundation for lasting peace and economic prosperity will be established when Sudan demonstrates that investment opportunities are not skewed to benefit only a section of the Sudanese community. Sierra Leone achieved this by implementing measures to combat illegal mining and promote sustainable practices. It also worked to improve transparency and accountability in the management of mineral resources.

Although Sierra Leone's journey to peace and prosperity was punctuated with multiple governance setbacks, it sustained peaceful transitions over the last two decades, demonstrating that Sudan, too, can outgrow its civil war and enjoy peace and prosperity. A lasting foundation is only laid when economic growth and prosperity are shared. Sierra Leone achieved this by implementing bottom-up models of economic development that empowered its people at the bottom of the pyramid.[127] I recommend that Sudan pursue the same approach, as this significantly contributed to averting the disillusionment of the masses.

Mozambique's Path to Stability

Mozambique endured a decade-long civil war that started in 1977, two years after they gained independence, and continued until 1992. The war was between the Mozambique Liberation Front *(Frente de Libertação de Moçambique,* or FRELIMO) and the Mozambican National Resistance *(Resistência Nacional Moçambicana,* or RENAMO). The seeds of war in the case of Mozambique, as well as Sudan, were sown by the divide-to-rule policy adopted in several African pre-colonial societies. The replica varies in degree, but the principle remains universal.

Mozambique's civil war took an ideological trajectory, pitting the ruling pro-Marxist party FRELIMO against an anti-Marxist coalition of small parties who fought either in parallel or alongside RENAMO.[128] The war was catalyzed by external forces that supported different factions, occasioned by regional interests that involved Zimbabwe and South Africa on one side and Tanzania and Zambia on the other.[129] Civilians bore the greatest brunt of the conflict as the warring parties targeted them, leading to mass displacement, over one million deaths, and widespread destruction of property.

Whereas the ceasefire was primarily the result of shifting regional dynamics and international pressure, the willingness of warring parties to de-escalate conflict saw the commencement of talks facilitated by a faith-based organization.[130] Following a protracted process of mediated negotiations, the parties achieved a ceasefire and agreed on a roadmap to stability, political reform, democracy, and the reintegration of former warriors in the society.[131]

The Mozambican case is a semi-perfect replica of Sudan and can be adopted as a leading example for Sudan's peace roadmap—with a few alterations to consider the contextual specificities of Sudan. Owing to Sudan's past and the length of the conflict, any peace efforts isolated from total reform of the political architecture and deep social stitching will not bear sustained peace.

Mozambique successfully put its legacy of civil war in the past because of the warring parties' commitment to political reforms, which paved the way for lasting stability and progress. Among these was the stipulation of elections under international supervision, devolution of power and governance, and support of the local authorities to ensure representation and participation at both grassroots and regional levels.[132]

Mozambique's journey to end civil war was anchored on protecting fundamental human rights and establishing accountable institutions, central to charting a new path to resilient peace.[133] The case of a ceasefire in Mozambique demonstrates that enduring a ceasefire is indeed possible in Sudan. This calls for the careful crafting of peace agreements founded on the philosophy of Sudanism. Beyond creating humanitarian corridors, an elaborate ceasefire agreement is necessary for Sudan to emerge from civil war and avert future conflicts. Peace agreements that pass the test of time include truth and reconciliation processes as part of the accord.

South Africa's Truth and Reconciliation

Truth, Justice, and Reconciliation (TJR) provides a mechanism for addressing past atrocities and other forms of injustice from the civil war. Its primary aim is to help heal wounds and reconcile affected populations. TJR has three components: truth establishment, justice delivery, and reconciliation. Truth-seeking aims to unearth and document the truth about past injustices and abuse through documentation of testimonies, investigations, and gathering evidence from victims and witnesses. This process may encompass public hearings, where people are given a chance to narrate their experiences. Depending on the agreed-upon mandate of the commission, it may recommend judicial actions against culprits, propose reparations to be accorded to victims, and set up mechanisms for enforcing the accountability of perpetrators for their actions. Such commissions can also accord amnesty to those who fully disclose the truth about their involvement in past abuses.

The fundamental aim of TJR is to foster the healing and reconciliation of conflict parties. The reconciliation component thus creates the chance for dialogue, promoting understanding between communities and groups and striving toward developing a more inclusive society.

Recommendations from the commission may include putting measures in place to restore victims' rights and prevent the reoccurrence of injustices. The Truth and Reconciliation Commission of South Africa (TRC) is one of the most well-known and influential examples of TJRs in Africa that Sudan can learn from.

South Africa's TRC was established under the African National Congress as a mechanism for healing following long years of racial discrimination. The Late President Nelson Mandela and the Late Archbishop Reverend Desmond Tutu played a catalytic role in the success of that commission. The TRC resulted from the negotiations and political reforms that led to the peaceful transition from racial segregation and discrimination to citizenship-driven democracy. Mandela's government took steps to tackle the human rights violations and injustices that constituted one of the more sickening legacies of the apartheid government.[134]

One of the foundational instruments to the success story of South Africa was the passing of the National Unity and Reconciliation Act of 1995.[135] The Act provided the legal framework for TRC's establishment. This means a similar commission must be established on a clear legal framework to be effective in Sudan. Also, the TRC process was entrusted to one of the most credible figureheads in South Africa's history, a prominent anti-apartheid activist and Nobel laureate, Archbishop Reverend Desmond Tutu. [136] Archbishop Tutu was instrumental in steering the TRC processes, shaping its approach, and guiding its work. For any such commission to be successful in the case of Sudan, it must be led by people of high integrity who can generate consensus among the population.

To earn local legitimacy and international respect, leaders of the Sudan Reconciliation Commission must be people with a record as vocal defenders of human rights, justice, and cohesion. If such people cannot be identified locally, international persons of high integrity and acceptability may be sourced.[137] It is noteworthy that while Mandela's government initiated the TRC, its establishment also resulted from significant grassroots advocacy efforts. The voices of civil society, activists, religious groups, and victims at the forefront of the fight against discrimination and segregation were pivotal in influencing the African National Congress (ANC) government to institute the commission. This means that collective political will and inclusive processes must be present for similar successes to be realized in Sudan.

In terms of structure, the TRC mandate was to address human rights violations during apartheid. The commission comprised three sub-committees: the Amnesty Committee, the Human Rights Violations Committee, and the Reparation and Rehabilitation Committee.

The Amnesty Committee handled applications from individuals who had committed politically motivated injustices during the apartheid era. This was conditional to fully disclosing their actions and demonstrating that only politics fueled the atrocities. This provided an opportunity for truth-telling without necessarily including forgiveness. Given the importance of truth-telling to the healing process, such a committee is essential in Sudan's quest for justice and reconciliation.

The Human Rights Violations Committee invited victims to narrate their experiences and provide evidence of the abuses suffered. Similarly, perpetrators were invited to testify and provide information about their actions.

The Reparation and Rehabilitation Committee was responsible for considering reparations for victims and making recommendations for rehabilitating individuals and communities affected by injustices. The focus of the Reparation and Rehabilitation Committee was to attend to the material, psychological, and symbolic dimensions of reparation.[136]

It may be argued that one of the inherent reasons for the TRC's success was the division of roles and allocation of responsibilities, which offered the needed agility to handle numerous cases efficiently and minimize the risk of mixing issues, enabling the TRC to execute its mandate seamlessly.[136]

South Africa's TRC held public hearings nationwide, where victims and perpetrators could testify and share their stories. Their process was transparent to the extent that the hearings were broadcast on TV and radio so that the nation could witness firsthand the extent of the abuses and leave no doubt about the impartiality and fairness of the process. Sudan can, therefore, adopt a similar, transparent process when constituting and implementing its version of TRC.[136]

South Africa's TRC significantly contributed to truth-seeking, acknowledgment, national healing, reconciliation, accountability, victim-centered approaches, and rebuilding trust and social cohesion. It played a crucial role in initiating a process of national healing and reconciliation. The TRC aimed to promote understanding, empathy, and forgiveness by allowing victims to be heard and perpetrators to confess their actions. The public nature of the TRC's hearings contributed to the collective recognition of the harm inflicted during apartheid and fostered a shared responsibility for reconciliation.

The TRC remains an essential model for truth and reconciliation that continues to inform transitional justice processes in various countries. Sudan must also benefit from this transitional justice success story. There is a rich literature on the TRC that concerned parties can borrow. Furthermore, some members of the TRC are alive and active and can be consulted on how they made the commission a story of success in South Africa.

Conclusion

In this chapter, I attempted to highlight parallels between the experiences of other countries that emerged from a history of civil war and the situation in Sudan to draw lessons from their success in breaking the vicious circle of internal conflicts. The case studies give hope that a new and sustainable peace path is possible for Sudan, despite its long history of internal turmoil. It will take robust, collaborative, and determined leadership to de-escalate the war in Sudan and chart a path toward healing the nation.

Peace in Sudan will become less elusive only when warring parties realize that war is a zero-sum game. One of the most viable paths toward resilient peace and prosperity in Sudan is the one that practices Sudanism as a national philosophy. As the cases of Rwanda, Angola, Sierra Leone, South Africa, and Mozambique have demonstrated, the buck stops with those who control the instruments of national power.

The preceding comparative analyses of five African cases demonstrate that transitioning to justice is not a quick-fix solution to peace in a country embroiled in civil war.

However, with the right policies, instruments, and political will, these cases provide a roadmap that is the best bet for Sudan's permanent break from the vicious circle of internal turmoil. This will require time, effort, and the collaboration of all.

In this chapter, I put forward practical ways in which Sudan can begin its turnaround toward a more stable future. The starting point is a commitment to peace through a firm determination that no internal war will ever be allowed to be fought in Sudan. This must be the first in a series of peace agreement agenda items incorporating a bottom-up framework for transitional justice. While the case studies discussed thus far offer gems of wisdom, I know they have not been without challenges.[138] However, even those challenges can be a crop of lessons for Sudan.

It is essential to advocate for the importance of the justice sector in post-conflict societies and highlight its role in ensuring accountability, promoting the rule of law, and preventing future conflicts. The roles of the international community, donors, and development partners are vital in providing financial and technical support for post-conflict justice delivery. Balancing competing priorities and allocating resources based on a comprehensive understanding of the needs of the society is paramount in achieving sustainable peace, justice, and development in post-conflict settings.[139] Collectively, these propositions constitute the basis for unpacking how Sudan can recover.

I reserve the subsequent chapters for prescriptions that could arrest or reverse the situation. The next chapter will delve into how to reverse Sudan's war cycle, where I propose practical policy-oriented action, including political leadership and governance, equity and socioeconomic development, professionalization of security apparatuses, regional and international cooperation, transitional justice and accountability, rebuilding the social fabric, and investing in education and empowerment.

In these subsequent discussions, I will be guided by the lessons learned from the African case studies discussed in the previous sections. I will also be guided by what I have learned from my interactions with friends, colleagues, elders, and leaders. This endeavor is a partially unguided walk in the wilderness. My guiding principles are candid, transparent, and an honest attempt to uplift Sudan from poverty and regression. Any fault of mine should not be taken as a premeditated attempt to misrepresent facts or situations. All counterarguments are invited so that we can enrich the debate together.

Chapter Six

REVERSING THE WAR CYCLE THROUGH POLICY ACTIONS

Introduction

In the introduction of this book, I argued that the outbreak of armed conflict in Sudan in April 2023 was the culmination of decades of degenerative, sociopolitical instability. As such, a lasting solution will not be possible without encompassing history and adopting a comprehensive approach to resolving the conflict, i.e., targeting the fire from its base. Given the compounded sentiments of injustice, negligence, and underdevelopment, one grants that achieving lasting peace in Sudan is a complex endeavor, but with concerted efforts and a comprehensive approach, it is undoubtedly attainable.

Sudan has experienced decades of internal conflicts requiring the resolution of multiple interrelated factors.[140] I draw from contextually relevant scholarly literature and explore key elements that could contribute to reversing the

Sudanese war cycle. These factors include political leadership and governance, equity in socioeconomic development, security apparatus professionalization, regional integration and cooperation, transitional justice and accountability, rebuilding the social fabric, and investing in education and empowerment.

Political Leadership and Governance

To break the cycle of military coups, conflicts, and wars, the Sudanese should unequivocally resolve that the mechanisms they agree on to end the conflict must stand the test of time and shape the country's path for the next three decades. Governance and political leadership—the umbrella term for this mandate—spans the precepts, practices, and framework through which choices will be made, policies developed, and public assets deployed.[76] Fundamentally, vision and direction will perhaps be the most critical leadership factor in pulling the country out of sludge to begin an orderly nation-building process.

Effective political leadership calls for an unclouded vision for Sudan, outlining the collective goals and aspirations for the future. Turnaround begins when those who wield the instruments of national power articulate a clear and compelling vision for a peaceful and prosperous future.[76] This vision should emphasize the benefits of peace, reconciliation, and unity, while highlighting the costs and consequences of continued conflict. It serves as a guiding framework to rally support and inspire citizens toward the common goal of lasting peace. The person of the moment leading this transition must have space for forgiveness, irrespective of what has happened.

A clear demarcation must be drawn around the war puzzle for Sudan to break with the past. One of the ways this can be done is by calling upon all the Sudanese to forgive each other. I am not suggesting unconditional forgiveness, as some reparation for the damage must take place to divorce emotions from the turbulent past. Several leading examples on the continent, such as the *Gacaca* courts in Rwanda and the Truth and Reconciliation Commission in South Africa, can be borrowed to deliver fair and compensatory forgiveness.

Having a vision alone cannot steer the country from the historical mess. Therefore, leaders need to show clear direction by dialoguing and negotiating with parties of the conflict to build consensus on the end state of peace. This is achievable by rooting for points of agreement and shared values and being responsive to the fears and misgivings of every stakeholder.[77] Tribalism, ethnicity, and racial abuses must be incriminated and faced with the full force of the law. Being Sudanese should be adopted as the sole condition for merit. If you are Sudanese, you are Sudanese with all the privileges and obligations of a national citizen. A free society is where citizens feel free and secure to exercise their religious practices and promote their cultures without retribution or intimidation.

Leaders have a social contract with the masses to advance policies that promote reconciliation and healing and foster understanding, forgiveness, and trust among parties in conflict. Effective policies on security sector reform ensure professionalization, accountability, and respect for human rights, while policies promoting inclusive governance ensure meaningful participation and representation for all segments of society.[141] Leaders should ensure mass support, leading by example and promoting inclusion and participation.[70]

Effective political leadership and governance after the civil war require a comprehensive approach to decision-making. I submit that leaders must adopt a conflict-sensitive perspective and make informed decisions that address the root causes of the conflict. Resilient peace requires addressing immediate humanitarian needs and tackling the underlying political dynamics, power imbalances, and resource distribution.[66] This approach calls for learning from past mistakes and adjusting decision-making to address immediate needs while focusing on structural reforms, institution-building, and reconciliation. In my view, these constitute the top priorities that the warring parties and mediators should pursue to address war grievances through well-designed policies and to erect a stable foundation for peace.[70]

Transparency and accountability in decisions and resource management are central to good governance. Political leaders ought to take responsibility for the policies and actions they pursue. I hold the view that this can be achieved when those at the helm of leadership subject themselves to public audits, create independent oversight bodies, and advocate for robust legal frameworks. Government institutions earn legitimacy when leaders are accountable and submit to the rule of law.[75]

Transparency and accountability act as deterrents against further conflicts by reining in the abuse of power, persons of evil character, and inequity in resource sharing. [142] Gone should be the days when a corrupt leader or public officer is rewarded, not only by being transferred to another location but often promoted. Likewise, the so-called favoritism, known as "*Wasta*," has been the source of many of Sudan's problems for decades. *Wasta* contributes to assigning responsibility to nonqualified persons whose sole merit is being connected with an influential person or affiliated with an organization. *Wasta* blocks qualified persons from being recruited, which amounts to a loss of valuable resources for the country.

Public participation is at the heart of political leadership. Political leaders should be seen encouraging public participation, soliciting feedback, and creating platforms for dialogue to ensure diverse perspectives are considered. Public participation in decision-making processes is vital in fostering lasting peace by creating a platform for diverse perspectives to be heard, addressing grievances, and building consensus. This inclusive approach enhances social cohesion and reconciliation by bringing together individuals from different backgrounds, facilitating dialogue, and fostering a shared vision for peace.[19]

Sudan's population is young, and, therefore, the energy of this youth must be absorbed in productive activities. They must be given secure platforms to dialogue and contribute to nation-building. The lack of proper channels for youth engagement only contributes to increasing the number of youths taking drugs, being radicalized, or idling around tea ladies, at best. Political leaders are equally responsible for facilitating inclusivity in dialoguing peace across different nation groups, from government representatives to leaders of different communities and individuals affected by civil war. They must be provided with a safe platform to express their sentiments, cross-fertilize different opinions, and identify common ground for the way forward.

Leadership must facilitate the provision of restitution as a symbolic gesture to those affected by the abuses and ensure that the wrongdoers demonstrate genuine remorse. The acknowledgment of past harms and provision of redress facilitate the healing of communities.[135] When leaders exemplify humility, followers will be more inclined to act likewise. Leaders' actions, more than words, transform societies. In contrast, when leaders preach virtue and practice otherwise, societies develop apathy to reform. At that point, leading a society to virtue becomes hugely challenging, if not impossible.

Equity in Socioeconomic Development

Restoring socioeconomic equity in the wake of civil war is a daunting but realistic task. As an important first step, I recommend that leaders prioritize providing essential services to all citizens irrespective of socioeconomic history. The latest war has destroyed most of the social infrastructure—which, admittedly, was in dilapidated shape even before the war began. Those entrusted with leadership on this front must collaborate with countries, institutions, and parties of goodwill to establish a humanitarian aid program to help meet essential needs, such as food, shelter, water, sanitation, and healthcare.

It is instructive to note that a country damaged to this extent cannot rely solely on aid to rebuild its infrastructure. Therefore, a clear investment plan must bring together efforts for local and foreign capital inflows. To that end, clear policies should be adopted to safeguard foreign investments and income repatriation without red tape and government bureaucracies.

Education is fundamental to the development of equity in the socioeconomic future of Sudan's post-conflict reconstruction. Leaders must build temporary schools or utilize community spaces for education to be effective and inclusive in such situations. Inclusive education is the only sustainable path out of poverty. Government should take full charge of education, and the tendency to proliferate private schools must be minimal. Providing free or subsidized education and promoting inclusive policies can help bridge the educational gap. This requires identifying and empowering marginalized groups and displaced individuals.

Those entrusted with Sudan's transition process should also encourage the active participation of marginalized groups in decision-making processes and provide them with opportunities for skill development, training, and entrepreneurship. This can help create more inclusive and equitable economic opportunities.[76] Leaders must establish and strengthen social protection systems to provide a safety net for vulnerable populations. This can include programs such as conditional cash transfers and healthcare subsidies.

These programs should be targeted to reach those most affected by the civil war, ensuring they are not left behind. This includes collaborating with Sudan partners to develop and implement programs that promote equity and socio-economic development.[143] Ensuring equity in socioeconomic development also calls for promoting transparency and accountability in managing resources and allocating aid. Leaders must establish mechanisms for oversight and monitoring to prevent corruption and ensure that resources reach those who need them the most.

During the short transition under Prime Minister Hamdok, the government initiated a social aid program known as "*Thamaraat*," or "fruits" in Arabic, in collaboration with the World Bank. The program was successful in alleviating economic burdens on households. Such programs can be resumed and improved to include helping poor households with production tools to develop small-scale productive activities.

Professionalization of Security Apparatus

It is an uphill task to professionalize the security system of a country experiencing civil turmoil, yet it is essential for achieving peace and stability. Professionalizing the security apparatus requires a comprehensive approach encompassing various security facets, ranging from recruitment and training to institutional development.

In my view, people entrusted to lead the process of professionalization of security should have an unobstructed vision of security, focused on their contribution to protecting the country, providing security to citizens, and following the rule of law. The vision should emphasize promoting human rights and performing duties with impartiality. The prolongation and multiplicity of the conflicts in Sudan yielded a deformed security structure that allowed for the proliferation of military ranks and decorations without merit.

It may not be hyperbole to say that Sudan has more generals than the US if you count all the generals of the various armed groups. It is cynical to see some generals in their early 30s. The only explanation would be that they were born in uniform. Some movements distributed high ranks to their officers in anticipation of potential reintegration into the army such that they could retain high military status post-integration. This is a sensitive matter and must be treated with utmost care to avert the renewal of the conflict. This can be done by forming an independent group of military experts to review the whole security apparatus structure and reposition military personnel into deserved ranks based on technical assessments, education, and years of service.

Second, those mandated to professionalize the security sector of Sudan should establish a clear leadership and command structure within the security apparatus. They should select leaders based on merit, experience, and a history of commitment to professionalism. They should be effective in instilling discipline and ethical conduct. Much talk has recently been had about reforming the Sudanese military ideology, but nothing has been accomplished thus far.

The military's top role in every country is to protect the country's interests, citizens, and sovereignty. The Sudanese army has figured prominently in the country's politics since independence. This is a structural deficiency in the army or the Sudanese political system. I recommend moving all army barracks outside civilian settlements as a first step. This requires massive investments, presenting a real test of the Sudan partners' will to help Sudan stabilize in the long term. Therefore, Special funds should be allocated to disarmament, reforming security, demobilizing personnel, reintegrating the demobilized, and relocating all security forces, except police, to settlements outside major cities.

Third, political leaders should be committed to reforming and strengthening security institutions, accountability, and oversight. There should be mechanisms for detecting and investigating misconduct and holding personnel accountable based on judicial impartiality. An essential aspect of ensuring this is fostering positive relationships between the security apparatus and local communities. I propose that leaders promote the community's involvement in security initiatives by fostering trust and cooperation through, among others, community policing.

The endeavor to professionalize the security system is a long-term aspiration that calls for continuous investment and perpetual commitment. It is imperative for leaders to continuously assess and adapt strategies to changing circumstances and allocate adequate resources for training, equipment, and institutional development.[144]

Regional and International Cooperation

Regional and international actors serve as peace facilitators and mediators who come in handy in de-escalating conflict and minimizing its implications on civilians. Regional actors are instrumental in post-conflict stability and reconstruction. They can be at the heart of diplomatic efforts to foster dialogue between conflicting parties.[86] This can include diplomatic visits, shuttle diplomacy, and the establishment of peace envoys or special representatives. Regional organizations like the AU, the IGAD, the EAC, and the LAS, in addition to the United Nations, provide opportunities and resources for peacekeeping and dialogue facilitation.

The Sudan partners' efforts are indispensable in supporting ceasefires, protecting civilians, and creating an environment that promotes the execution of peace accords. International and regional organizations have been instrumental in restoring stabilities in Liberia, Sierra Leone, and many other African countries that experienced similar turmoil. As peacekeepers, regional and international actors should provide stabilizing forces, establish safe spaces for bringing warring parties together, and secure humanitarian activities. Cooperation is required to coordinate activities, including but not limited to providing healthcare and food to populations affected by the civil war.

For this effort to be orderly and effective, I call for mobilizing Sudan's advocacy campaign and creating a global network of former diplomats, Sudanese scholars, and businesspeople to initiate a worldwide movement to support Sudan in reconstruction efforts. The advocacy groups should mobilize financial resources and technical expertise to implement the most urgent recovery programs and help the transitional administration sail through transitional challenges.

Transitional Justice and Accountability

Transitional justice is one of many mechanisms designed to address the historical challenges of countries transitioning from conflict. It focuses on restoring the rule of law by addressing historical injustices to lay a firm foundation for a fair future. The goal is to end lawlessness, re-establish the rule of law in countries emerging from civil war, and address war crimes to help achieve lasting peace.[145] Transitional justice is motivated by the need to reconcile with a turbulent past, reverse trends of social marginalization, and end impunity. It seeks to nurture social trust, mend fractured relations, and promote peaceful coexistence.[146]

Transitioning to justice from conflict begins with a ceasefire as the crucial first step, followed by a series of actions to achieve sociopolitical stability.[147] This is a typical endeavor of any country embroiled in civil war. [148] Transitional justice takes two distinct but complementary trajectories: judicial and non-judicial.

The judicial trajectory includes criminal prosecutions and investigating the fate of disappeared persons, while non-judicial paths encompass truth commissions, reparations programs, and commemorative practices. Institutional reforms also constitute one of the non-judicial archetypes of transition to justice. Institutional reforms are sequenced post-delivery of transitional justice and include reforming the security and judiciary sectors, constituting fundamental aspects of resilient peace.

Transitional justice is inspired by the realization that victims and survivors of past atrocities and injustices in post-conflict societies do not forget what has happened to them. If their experiences remain unaddressed and are allowed to fester, they will have catastrophic consequences in the future. The children who grow up in war will experience life-long traumatization and will not transition into productive members of society.

Attempts to evade the reality of those who have suffered hideously in the past set the stage for those memories to explode in violent response to the immediate present. Further, the memory of these realities is transmitted to future generations and becomes a mythology that sparks even more vehement reactions in the future.

Transitional justice recognizes victims' rights to justice as a necessary precursor to peace, without which peace would merely be a brief interlude between conflicts. In this book, I use the analogy of a raging fire to represent conflict. The best way to put out a fire eternally is to target the firebase, i.e., to address the problem at its roots. If only the flames were addressed and the slumbering coals were not doused with a fire extinction agent, live coals would remain, waiting for an opportunistic wind to rekindle a fire even deadlier and more challenging to control. As a result, a nation finds itself in a vicious cycle of population displacement, destruction of property, human rights abuses, and death. This has been the ugly history of Sudan since independence.

Transitional justice mechanisms will help Sudan forge a peaceful path forward, heal broken hearts, and help people reconcile with their tragic pasts. The appropriate conviction is that lasting peace is only achievable if the perpetrators of human rights abuses are brought to book, and victims are materially and morally healed.[148]

One important aspect of transitional justice is uncovering the truth about past human rights violations. This can involve establishing truth commissions or similar bodies to investigate and document the abuses committed during the conflict.[145] I submit that leaders in Sudan should maintain the obligation to hold the culprits accountable for their crimes by agreeing on and establishing a transitional justice system to bring such culprits to account. Subjecting such individuals to a fair judicial procedure prevents future impunity.[112] Impartiality is imperative to avoid witch hunts or mob justice. Quite often, when people give up on prospects of equitable justice, they try to do justice themselves.

Transitional justice is also about recognizing victims of injustices and offering reparation to them. Multiple forms of reparation can be implemented, such as monetary compensation, medical care, rehabilitation of communities, provision of education facilities, and memorialization. These initiatives aim to address the harm caused by the conflict and contribute to the healing and rebuilding of affected communities.[112] In my view, these actions are among the very least that leaders can utilize to restore dignity to victims of the atrocities in Sudan.

The worst form of injustice is violence against women, especially rape. No form of material reparation can compensate victims of sexual abuse. Rape is an inhumane act beyond all boundaries of imagination. Perpetrators of this abject form of punishment are fully aware of the long-term emotional pain it causes, and they use it deliberately to inflict the maximum possible pain on the victims and their loved ones. In my view, rape is an unforgivable crime and must be punished. The only solace for rape victims is to see the perpetrator facing the full force of the law.

Reconciliation processes are also essential for healing divisions in Sudan. I propose that leaders take deliberate actions to foster dialogue, promote understanding, and facilitate encounters between victims and perpetrators. We must be cognizant that implementing transitional justice during an ongoing civil war can be complex and challenging. As such, prioritizing the most critical aspects and adapting processes to the dynamics on the ground may be necessary.[76]

As mentioned earlier, there are numerous examples across Africa and beyond that Sudan can follow to ensure best practices are adopted and implemented. Implementing restorative justice mechanisms alongside retributive justice can help repair relationships and address the harm caused by conflicts. Restorative justice approaches focus on repairing the harm done to individuals and communities and seek to involve all stakeholders in the resolution process. Reparations to victims can also contribute to rebuilding trust and facilitating socioeconomic recovery.[76]

Rebuilding the Social Fabric

Rebuilding the social fabric of Sudan is a critical aspect of post-conflict reconstruction and peacebuilding. It involves addressing the deep divisions, grievances, and mistrust that result from the conflict. Facilitating dialogue and reconciliation processes that bring together diverse groups affected by the conflict is crucial.

I therefore recommend that those entrusted with leading this process create safe spaces for dialogue as part of a broader effort to promote understanding and foster empathy between different ethnic, religious, and political communities. Acknowledging the past and confronting historical narratives is essential for healing and reconciliation.[149] Engaging civil society organizations, community leaders, and grassroots initiatives can help bridge divides and build trust. [150]

Restitching the social fabric starts at the community level. Leaders should support community-led initiatives that promote healing, trust-building, and cooperation. They can achieve this by prioritizing projects focused on trauma healing, intergroup dialogue, cultural exchanges, and joint development efforts. They should emphasize shared values, common goals, and mutual understanding to accelerate the rebuilding of relationships and foster social cohesion.

This should not be a challenging endeavor in Sudan, given the existence of a solid, hierarchical, popular administrative system known as *"Al-Idara Al-Ahlia."* The popular administrative system is structured and divided based on tribal land demarcations and has been well maintained since the colonial era. Authorities should involve *Al-Idara Al-Ahlia* in this process. However, this should be done transparently to avert further inter-tribal alienations.

It is crucial to acknowledge that reconstructing the social fabric is a long-term endeavor that calls for continuous commitment, investment, and patience. I emphasize local relevance, and this should consider the nuanced dynamics of local communities.[149] Sudan partners' support, including financial assistance, technical expertise, and capacity-building, can significantly contribute to these efforts. Ultimately, the involvement and ownership of local communities are critical to a successful reconstruction of the social fabric.[145]

Investing in Education and Empowerment

Education and empowerment should be prioritized in the agenda of post-conflict Sudan. Sudan's long-term peace and prosperity depend on the education of its people and their sense of empowerment.[151] Education is vital to the productivity of a nation, an indispensable empowerment tool, and an engine for sustainable growth. An educated and empowered people constitute the most needed input factor for reconstruction.

I emphasize *inclusivity* in quality education and empowerment, especially to marginalized groups and those displaced by the conflict. This not only promotes peace but lays the proper foundation for socioeconomic development. Educators should prioritize developing inclusive and peace-oriented curricula that promote tolerance, respect for diversity, and conflict-resolution skills. This calls for the incorporation of reconciliation ethos toward the promotion of social cohesion and peace. Local communities should actively participate in curriculum development to ensure cultural relevance and sensitivity.

Investment in teacher training programs for delivering relevant education in post-conflict Sudan is imperative. Such training should adopt teaching processes that focus on trauma healing and are sensitive to conflict. There should be intentionality in providing psychological safety to learners by creating a safe space for self-expression.

Curriculum stability should be maintained to ensure the interconnection of the education ladder across generations. A critical factor contributing to the deterioration of the education system in Sudan is regular curriculum changes. This is not rocket science. If you change curriculum twice in 10 years, you risk tearing a generation apart and breaking down knowledge transfer. The education curriculum should not be altered so frequently or thoughtlessly.

The status of teachers must be elevated, and their salaries and benefits must be fundamentally restructured. Teachers in Sudan are among the lowest paid, making the teaching job a last resort for those lacking lucrative options. Teachers are role models and partners in raising future generations. A teacher unable to dress decently and struggling to commute to school will not have much to offer. Poorly dressed teachers are looked down upon by society and by their students. The government must increase teachers' salaries, introduce distinct uniforms, and provide transportation services, housing schemes, and subsidized cooperatives where a teacher can satisfy life necessities and live decently.

From an educational lens, empowerment encompasses providing vocational skills development to the youth and adult victims of conflict. Such skills can then be deployed to the rebuilding of communities. When the youth are engaged in gainful employment because they have marketable skills, they not only contribute to post-conflict reconstruction, but their economic engagement reduces their chances of recruitment into activities of lawlessness.

The previous government in Sudan introduced what it termed the "Higher Education Revolution," which resulted in the opening of around 25 higher education institutions within a brief time span. While this was considered a progressive approach toward securing equity in education, the downside of the program is that it contributed to high levels of involuntary unemployment, as the number of graduates exceeded the labor market absorption capacity by far, resulting in a deformed labor market to the extent that university graduates ended up competing for all sorts of manual jobs.

I encountered cases where graduates ended up being fast-food delivery staff, taxi drivers, or open-market hawkers. With limited employment options and a bleak outlook, they had to find ways to make a living while being hopeful for a miracle somewhere on the horizon. To that end, they carried their certificates everywhere they went, hoping they could stumble onto unexpected opportunities.

Conclusion

In this chapter, I explored the foundational factors for resilient peace in Sudan. It is important to note that these factors are interconnected and should be addressed comprehensively rather than in isolation. Resilient peace requires a long-term commitment from all stakeholders, including the government, civil society, regional actors, and the Sudan partners.

While commitment is an essential first step, reversing the cycle of war is a complex and multifaceted process that requires more than just commitment. It involves addressing underlying causes of conflict, promoting inclusive governance, ensuring equitable access to resources, promoting justice and accountability, fostering social and economic development, and building community trust. Sustained engagement and cooperation among stakeholders are necessary to navigate potential setbacks and challenges.

Sudan can increase the likelihood of achieving resilient peace and creating a more stable and prosperous future by fostering a collaborative and inclusive approach. Accordingly, in the concluding chapter, I turn attention to the core objective of the book, which is to draw a recovery roadmap for Sudan. I draw a 12-point recovery agenda, which I classify into immediate, intermediate, and long-term actions.

Chapter Seven

REVERSING THE WAR CYCLE TO A RECOVERY PATH

Introduction

Can Sudan emerge from the vicious cycle of military coups, armed conflicts, and economic underperformance? Yes, but conditionally. Breaking the vicious cycle takes more than well wishes, prayers, and political slogans. It requires three things: first, admitting that a real problem exists; second, a firm belief that the Sudanese deserve a better future; and third, practical actions to divorce from past errors and build the desirable future.

The first two fundamentals—confession and belief—require a nationwide move supported by intellectuals and orchestrated by a visionary leader. Only under such a leader can the Sudanese pray that God will bless Sudan with a better future. The third fundamental—practical actions—is a technical endeavor that can be formulated, funded, and implemented with the concerted efforts of Sudan and its partners. My role, and that of my fellow scholars and thinkers, is to help charter this path by contributing ideas, sharing technical expertise, and disseminating the experiences of other nations that have overcome comparable hurdles.

In this chapter, I contribute to Sudan's recovery vision by proposing a 12-point agenda to lay the foundation for a peaceful and sustainable future. These are divided into three sub-agendas that I refer to here as *action groups* based on relative urgency. These are immediate actions, intermediate actions, and long-term actions.

Immediate actions include ceasing the war, negotiating an agreement, forming a government of national unity, and charting a path to elections. Intermediate actions comprise integrating the armed forces, securing a process that achieves transitional justice, building a resilient peace, and developing a reliable social infrastructure. Long-term actions cover the transformation of the education system, relocation of the capital city, abolishing tribalism, and taking baby steps toward reintegration of Sudan and South Sudan under mutually acceptable arrangements.

I emphasize that these action groups are not necessarily sequential but could be overlapping and parallel. This means that several sub-agenda items can be tackled concurrently, while others may be prioritized based on the unfolding situation, as assessed by the people and organizations tasked with implementing the 12-point agenda.

Immediate Recovery Actions

Immediate actions include ending the war, negotiating an agreement, forming a national unity government, and charting a path to elections. These four action points are discussed next.

- *Ending the War*

No war lasts forever. Ongoing conflicts in Sudan will eventually become history. The fighting will stop because of war fatigue, if not through negotiations and good hearts. Yes, fighting will stop automatically or through external actions. But war will not stop for good if the root causes are not addressed. The fighting between RSF and SAF is a culmination and manifestation of the failure of the Sudanese to accommodate each other, acknowledge past mistakes, and have a forward-looking view of how a nation should be built and sustained. Ending the war requires a nationwide convention on peaceful resolution of current and future conflicts. It means that people should agree on house rules to resolve their differences—not through violence and guns, but through democratic means.

Ending the war means an irreversible agreement that no future armed conflict should be allowed on the land. Each previous conflict ended with a ceasefire sand peace agreement, but because ending-the-war status was not reached, another conflict broke out, requiring another ceasefire. Only ending the war can lead to a lasting ceasefire, not vice versa. Democracy provides a healthy environment for people to express their differences and elect their leaders, and has inherent tools that enable citizens to get rid of bad ones. Therefore, only democracy can sustain the peaceful expression of ideas and resolve differences.

The case studies discussed in the previous chapter demonstrate that the nations of Mozambique, Sierra Leone, and Angola only ended conflict and resumed development after establishing peaceful methods of power alternation. Sudan should, therefore, aim to establish a democratic process for political practice and agree on a constitution subjected to a referendum. This is a critical step that should not be delayed any further. Nonetheless, it remains an option for the Sudanese to agree on timing and sequencing to achieve the process that leads to ending the war.

Alongside the efforts to stop the fighting and end the war, humanitarian response to the plight of affected populations is the most essential and immediate action point for any nation that emerges from an armed conflict. For this action point to be practical, it must be governed by a set of principles in accordance with humanitarian standards that include humanity, neutrality, impartiality, and independence.[152]

The principle of humanity aims to save lives and alleviate people's suffering, notwithstanding their allegiances or affiliations. The principle of neutrality means that humanitarian actors must remain neutral and impartial, providing assistance based on needs alone, without taking sides in the conflict.[153] The principle of impartiality is about equal access to aid. It means humanitarian response should be seen to be unbiased and non-discriminatory. The principle of independence means that humanitarian response should be free from political, economic, or military interests.[154]

You cannot begin talking about peace while someone somewhere keeps firing gunshots or holding a gun to your forehead. It is as simple as that. Silencing the gun is a fundamental first step to peace. Guns and logic are two separate and mutually exclusive ways of communication. One communicates by either using bullets or agreeing to put the gun down and talk, not talking while firearms are brandished.

One of the most ironic things happening in most conflicts is that warring parties are always keen to leverage their respective military strength to extract concessions during negotiations. Hence, the most intense fighting happens during the last moments before the negotiation begins. This is total nonsense. Peace comes from the heart, not from a gun barrel.

Fighting to gain territory before negotiations indicates that warring parties are not prepared for peace since they intend to continue fighting more fiercely should negotiations fail. Deliberately or inadvertently, the fate of the negotiation will have been decided even before its commencement. This means that peace is no more than a plan B for the warring parties, while their plan A is to crush the adversary. There is simply no hope for a transition to justice without a ceasefire.[155] However, a ceasefire should not be taken as a temporary suspension of hostilities between warring parties, but out of a genuine desire to build and sustain peace. Unfortunately, this is not always the case because, often, warring parties know well how to capitalize on the fact that mediators are more concerned with the fate of the civilian population trapped in war, and therefore, they adopt a form of rent-seeking behavior: holding civilians at ransom.

A more potent approach that is a deterrent and persuader may be needed. The current deterrent measures imposed on war antagonists, such as asset freezes and travel bans, are clearly not efficient enough deterrents. If you stop the shelling and allow troops and assets to be moved around, you are only helping the warring parties to reposition, restock, recruit, and prepare for a more prolonged conflict.

In the case of Sudan, the warring parties must agree to halt combat and create an environment favorable for dialogue and potential resolution of the issues at the heart of the conflict. Warring parties must stop all forms of aggression, including armed movements. Observers with adequate knowledge of Sudan know well that while a ceasefire can be achieved by extracting a commitment from the warring parties' leaders, a sustained resolution to the crisis requires including what I term in this book as *war benchers*.

Each warring party has one or more political incubators, the fundamental forces behind the war. They are the base of the fire. The Generals are no more than flames. These incubators are the beak of the monster. In the conflict between SAF and RSF, the mediators—the US and Saudi Arabia—attempted a temporary humanitarian truce in Jeddah 10 times, which was violated every time. It could well be the case that the generals have a genuine desire to halt firing, but other forces think otherwise. While this has failed in the past, warring parties must realize that continued fire exchange means losses for every party.

On the other hand, a ceasefire offers immediate relief to the population by reducing the loss of lives and halting the destruction of property. Cessation of hostilities creates an environment more favorable for justice processes to commence. With a ceasefire, warring parties can agree to come to the negotiating table and begin addressing the grievances that sparked the conflict. Agreeing to a ceasefire has political value to warring parties because it makes them come across as sensitive to the humanitarian needs of affected populations.

Warring parties will contribute to an essential aspect of justice by allowing humanitarian aid to affected communities. By extension, this can build trust and confidence as the conflicting parties recognize that the other side is committed to stopping hostilities. This can foster trust, providing a much-needed window of opportunity for transitional justice. Ceasefire creates stability and security for subsequent steps and mechanisms to begin.

- *Negotiate an Agreement*

Negotiating an agreement following a civil war is a complex and delicate process.[156] This begins with recognizing that there are underlying human needs behind the hardline stances adopted by warring parties. Often, these needs are core to dignity: the need to exercise agency and control one's fate, the need to be recognized and valued, the need to belong, and the need for meaningful purpose in life. Advancement of these shared needs and creative reconciliation of different interests is part of the art of negotiation.[157] Below, I draw out the basic steps that peace talks should follow. These steps include establishing a framework, building a foundation for trust, identifying and prioritizing the key issues, facilitating the dialogue, drafting a comprehensive agreement, and enforcing and monitoring the agreement.[158]

Establishing a framework constitutes creating a neutral and inclusive forum where representatives from all sides can come together to discuss and resolve their differences. The framework should define the scope and objectives of the negotiations, the timeline, and the rules of engagement.

Building a foundation for trust calls for participants to see themselves as working side by side to attack the problem rather than attacking each other. It means seeing conflicting parties not as adversaries but as analytical people. Emphasis must be put on conducting negotiations in a way that will promote rather than hinder future negotiations. This includes giving and taking to arrive at some mutually agreeable middle ground. Conflicting parties must be encouraged, even pressured, to cede some ground in exchange for some gains from each other.

Identifying and prioritizing the key issues is considered critical to peace talks. An understanding of what is at stake often lays a firm foundation for arriving at a win-win agreement. Negotiators should prioritize dealing with people's issues end to end. This calls for disentangling the people from the problem, focusing on interests rather than positions, inventing multiple options for mutual gain before deciding, and insisting that the outcome of negotiations be based on an objective standard. Understanding the fears of each party is essential to finding common ground.

Facilitating the dialogue allows all parties to express their viewpoints and concerns. This process should ensure the representation of the different stakeholders and the participation of minority groups and civil society. Facilitators of negotiation must encourage open and honest communication while providing a safe space for discussions. Mediators or facilitators can be crucial in guiding the negotiations and helping parties find common ground. In this respect, the Sudan partners can provide credibility, resources, and expertise to the negotiation process. Sudan partners can also help ensure the implementation and enforcement of the agreement.

Drafting a comprehensive agreement that outlines the terms and commitments of all parties involved must follow once consensus is reached on the key issues. The agreement should address the underlying causes of the conflict, provide mechanisms for dispute resolution, and establish a roadmap for implementing the agreed-upon reforms.

Mechanisms for enforcing and monitoring the agreement must be instituted by establishing an Independent Joint Monitoring Commission (IJMC) supported by the Sudan partners. The IJMC will be mandated to provide oversight of the peace accord's negotiation and implementation. Such a commission must be the pivotal point of contact for all parties.

- ### Form an Agile Government of National Programs

Part of the mandate of the IJMC must be to facilitate on-going negotiation to establish an Agile Government of National Programs (AGNP). The proposed government should be agile in that it is formed from a compact list of ministries with time-sensitive deliverables to act swiftly and make its presence felt on the ground. It should also have a specifically tailored program to deliver the transition and adapt the country for lasting political stability.

The AGNP is comparable with the post-conflict Transitional Government of National Unity (TGNU). I propose and recommend AGNP as a variant of the TGNU customized for Sudan. The only difference between the TGNU and the AGNP is that the AGNP should be formed from technocrats and independent persons and not be subjected to power-sharing considerations to the extent that this is possible.

Politicians who opt to take roles at the AGNP should not be allowed to participate in post-transition politics to avoid conflicts of interest. Instead, all political parties vying for political representation should consolidate their effort to either win the democratic elections or merge with other political parties to garner political influence after the elections. This is crucial because the transitional period should be entirely devoted to rebuilding national institutions, improving the social infrastructure, consolidating the peace process, and laying the foundations for a nation-state.

No time should be wasted during the brief transition period on political disputes. As evidence has shown in several instances, including during the Prime Minister Hamdok government and the transition period leading to South Sudan's secession, endless political contestations divert government resources from the core objectives of nation-building to political disputes.

The AGNP should have, as part of its mandate, the task of midwifing Sudanism as the guiding philosophy for post-conflict reconstruction and the long-term transformation of the country. Because conflict erupts over who should rule the country rather than how the country should be ruled, both are important facets that must be considered in restoring stability. I propose four fundamental principles that will take care of both. In order of priority, these principles are formation of agile government, transitional justice, institutional reforms, and affirmative actions in post-conflict reconstruction.

Agile government: While the prime minister and deputy prime minister may be chosen based on charisma and experience, the transitional administration should be formed from young men and women. I recommend the adoption of new cabinet naming systems that do not include the term "minister." I submit that Sudan requires fresh thinking and an innovative approach, just short of revolutionary, to break away from the repetitive failures of the past. Youth have energy and fresh ideas and are less contaminated by historical politics, ideology, ethnicity, and tribalism. Yes, they might have their own views of the current situation, but they are not part of the historic failures that Sudan has experienced for the last 67 years.

The 2019 peaceful revolution was led by the youth, as we all know. The level of orderliness and organization of the peaceful demonstration was overwhelming. The leaders of the peaceful uprising maintained focus despite provocations, arrests, and killings. They painted bright pictures of the faithful Sudan as it should be. They did not neglect culture despite running battles with security forces. They turned the sit-in location into beautiful artwork—producing creative murals, writing powerful lyrics and songs, caring for each other, and raising funds from members' contributions. In short, they demonstrated unmatched organization, advocacy, and mobilization prowess. They mastered all the prerequisites of efficient miniature government. Sadly, their entire effort was usurped by politicians who resurfaced after victory had been declared.

Transitional justice: The established Agile Government of National Programs (AGNP) must institute accountability, truth-telling, and justice mechanisms to address human rights abuses committed during the civil war. The AGNP focuses on reconciliation and healing in the aftermath of civil war by addressing grievances, promoting dialogue, and fostering social cohesion. This does not mean the Independent Joint Monitoring Commission (IJMC) will have outlived its usefulness. Instead, the AGNP can transform IJMC into a Truth, Justice, and Reconciliation Commission (TJRC) with a fresh mandate to oversee the transitional justice process.

The commission should establish grassroots courts, like Rwanda's *Gacaca* courts, to promote truth-telling, reconciliation, and accountability by allowing community members to come forward and testify about the crimes committed and for the accused to confess their actions. A culturally relevant equivalent can help restore victims of atrocities and heal their wounds in Sudan.

Institutional reforms: Institutional reform is a key principle of establishing an AGNP. Lasting unity cannot be anchored on institutional vehicles purported to have facilitated injustices and atrocities. Among the conditions of a ceasefire must be mechanisms for an intentional and systematic process of reforming the structures, procedures, policies, and practices of governing institutions to make them more accountable and effective in serving the needs of citizens. Reforms must target state institutions—from security forces to the judiciary and public administration—and include mechanisms to address corruption and power transfer.

Affirmative action in post-conflict reconstruction: The root cause of civil conflict is often the result of years of marginalization in economic development. Addressing socio-economic inequalities that contributed to the conflict must be at the top of the AGNP's itinerary. Clear policies and implementation frameworks must accompany post-conflict economic reconstruction, focusing on growth stimulation in neglected areas.

Sudan formed some semblance of an AGNP following the 2019 popular uprising and the ousting of President Omar Al-Bashir. This did not live up to its promise, as demonstrated by the recent outbreak of armed conflict.[159] However, it must also be noted that weak institutions partly contributed to this regression because the transition was not accompanied by adequate capacity development.

The transitional government of 2019 was subjected to political power-sharing by allocating cabinet portfolios to political parties and resistance movements. It was amazing how the political practice during that transition focused on distributing the eggplant before it was roasted. In other words, political activists were only interested in grabbing ministerial positions, even though the political system was yet to be solidified. I wonder what sense it makes to prioritize securing political ambitions when people die of hunger and curable diseases. To me, the political position should come in voluntarily as a recompense for genuine efforts in people's service. It should be a call to duty, not a fight for fame.

It does not help the transition when the administration focuses on dealing with differences among its members rather than looking at the bigger picture. Politicians wasting time on power allocation disputes while ignoring national interests is like wild dogs fighting over partially incapacitated prey. By the time they settle their fight, the prey may have recovered and escaped into the wilderness.

One observable trend in less-developed political systems is that political practice is viewed as a means for making a living. It is an employment prospect for the jobless. It is the fastest and easiest way to get rich and accomplish financial security. A political position benefits the person taking the position and extends to the close family, extended family, clans, friends, and neighbors. In Sudan, the act of becoming a minister is sometimes considered a goal rather than a means to serve the people. It attracts political power and social influence. The entourages around the *"Maali Al-Wazir,"* an Arabic term for "Excellency the Minister," secure business opportunities, tender awards, and wide-open government doors—in other words, near-universal favorable treatment. The perception of a political job as a means of securing one's future must fundamentally change to one destined to serve the electorate. This is one of the reasons I authored this book, where I propose a drastic reconstitution of the political architecture in Sudan.

■   *Chart a Path to Elections*

Sudan will have completed its transformational journey by conducting free, fair, and credible elections. However, conducting a free and fair election in a country emerging from civil war is complex and challenging.[160] It requires careful planning, organization, and stakeholder commitment. The first step is creating an independent and impartial commission overseeing the electoral process.

An Independent Electoral and Boundaries Commission (IEBC) is a body established in some countries to oversee the electoral process and delimitation of electoral boundaries. The primary role of an IEBC is to ensure that elections are conducted fairly, transparently, and following the laws and regulations of the country. Additionally, the commission is responsible for defining and reviewing electoral boundaries to ensure equitable representation and distribution of political power.

In Kenya, for instance, one of the significant reforms in the aftermath of the worst post-election violence in the country's history was the establishment of the IEBC as part of the promulgation of a new constitution in 2010. The IEBC was created to replace the previous Electoral Commission of Kenya, which had been perceived as lacking independence and credibility. The IEBC oversees all electoral processes in Kenya, including voter registration, conducting elections, and delimiting electoral boundaries. It comprises a team of commissioners appointed through a rigorous and transparent process to ensure their independence from political interference.

The establishment of the IEBC was a significant step toward promoting fair and transparent elections in Kenya and rebuilding public trust in the electoral process. Kenya's IEBC represented a significant milestone in its journey toward political maturity. Sudan's IEBC should be composed of individuals with integrity and credibility to gain the trust of all parties involved. The commission is responsible for organizing and conducting distinct types of elections, such as presidential, parliamentary, local government, and referenda. It should also be tasked with defining and reviewing electoral boundaries for constituencies, wards, or other administrative units.

The commission may work with local and international observers to monitor the electoral process for transparency and fairness. It must be free from political interference and influence to maintain public trust in the electoral process. The AGNP should create electoral laws to safeguard the commission's independence and ensure its members are non-partisan and appointed transparently.

The IEBC should launch voter education campaigns to inform citizens about the electoral process, their rights and responsibilities, and the importance of participating in the election. This is especially crucial in post-conflict settings where people might have limited knowledge of democratic processes. The commission should encourage media freedom and fair reporting to allow citizens to make informed decisions. It should also encourage diverse representation among candidates and ensure that all population segments are adequately represented. This can help address historical grievances and foster national reconciliation.

Mechanisms must be put in place for a smooth post-election transition. Many countries have a transitional committee that oversees the process from the incumbent structure to the newly elected government. The goal of a transitional committee is to create a seamless transfer of leadership, minimizing disruptions and maximizing the effectiveness of the new administration from day one. The committee helps maintain stability and continuity within the organization or government by providing essential support and guidance during this critical period.

Intermediate Recovery Actions

Intermediate actions comprise integrating the armed forces, securing a process for transitional justice, building a resilient peace, and developing a reliable social infrastructure. These four action points are discussed next.

- *Integrate the Armed Forces*

The (re)deployment and integration of diverse armed groups—both regular armies and paramilitary groups—into a unified armed force following a ceasefire from civil war is a complex and delicate process. Several vital steps are required to ensure a smooth transition. The various armed groups must agree to not only merging their personnel but also the arms units and arsenals at the disposal of each party in a transparent and accountable manner. This plan should outline the collection, control, and disposal of weapons each side holds.[161] Under the circumstances Sudan finds itself in, peacekeeping forces must oversee this process to ensure compliance. This can involve merging units, thus fostering a sense of unity and a shared sense of purpose.[162]

For the effective functioning of the armed forces following a ceasefire, there must also be a robust command and control structure with transparent reporting and communication channels. The security sector, including the military, must reform to address any underlying issues contributing to the civil war. This may involve restructuring the military command structure, vetting personnel, and implementing measures to ensure accountability and adherence to human rights standards. Most importantly, capacity development should adopt a long-term view and, as such, establish mechanisms for sustained commitment and investment.

The established AGNP should create a framework for the progressive disarmament and (re)deployment of combatants. This process must be transparent, both procedurally and in distribution, and ensure checks and balances to safeguard the process from potential opportunistic tendencies that aim to advance selfish political interests. This is done to ensure that no side enjoys preferential treatment, to reduce grievances, and to confer equity between the armed groups. The framework must also include a transitional justice measure to respond to grievances and foster reconciliation within the disciplined forces.

For the merger process to be successful, there is a need for an independent body tasked with monitoring and verification of compliance with agreed-upon procedures and standards. This should facilitate confidence building, mitigate the risk of rearming the parties, and resolve potential violations. Again, in collaboration with trusted local actors, Sudan partners should be instrumental in this process. International support, diplomatic efforts, and sustained engagement are necessary to realize resilient peace.

- *Secure a Process for Transitional Justice*

Capacity development, especially for a bottom-up approach to transitional justice, is crucial for fostering sustainable and inclusive processes that address the needs and aspirations of affected communities in order to avert a repeat of future conflict. On this front, the Sudan partners should help strengthen capacity by empowering local actors, adopting participatory methodologies, providing legal and technical expertise, and fostering resource mobilization.

Capacity development should underscore the significance of empowering local communities, civil society organizations, grassroots movements, and other relevant stakeholders. These should be provided with the knowledge, skills, and resources necessary to participate in transitional justice processes. In the spirit of Sudanism, an appeal to join should be extended to the competent Sudanese in the diaspora. Policies promoting citizen participation and resource devolution must be implemented, empowering local communities to take charge of their own development.[163]

Since the Sudan partners play a crucial role in fostering capacity development, emphasis should be put on participatory methodologies that enable affected communities to engage in decision-making processes actively. These can encompass, among other things, community consultations, community-based research, and participatory mapping exercises.

Capacity development efforts should support the adoption and implementation of these methodologies. This also promotes implementing context-specific approaches to affirmative action rather than imposing a one-size-fits-all model. Sudan must build local actors' legal and technical expertise through training and apprenticeship in transitional justice mechanisms, human rights law, documentation, evidence gathering, victim support, and conflict resolution.[164]

The established AGNP, collaborating closely with Sudan partners, is responsible for supporting local actors in accessing the necessary resources to implement bottom-up transitional justice initiatives. This may include providing guidance on project proposal writing, facilitating connections with funding organizations, or exploring alternative funding mechanisms. Building financial sustainability and resource mobilization skills is essential for the long-term success of capacity development efforts.

▪ *Build a Resilient Peace*

Lasting peace and stability in Sudan can only be guaranteed when leaders are intentional about it. Hence, I argue that achieving sustainable peace is a priority in building a more resilient Sudan. But what does a resilient Sudan look like? One of the arguments I advance is that at the post-crisis stage, those who lost their loved ones might grieve their loss for many years, those physically harmed by the conflict may nurse their injuries for extended durations, and those maimed may spend their post-conflict life with a permanent disability.[165] Even those who escaped harm but witnessed the atrocities may experience vicarious trauma. Among these are first responders to distress calls, healthcare professionals, and family members of civil war casualties. The AGNP must be alive to this reality in its quest to build a more resilient Sudan.

I intimated this in my prescription for *"ending the war."* My point here is to argue that post-conflict healing is not a short-term undertaking. As such, it is vital to anchor post-crisis resilience on a set of fundamental tenets. I derive specific qualities that should constitute the tenets of resilient peace moving forward.

The first tenet is recovery, which is restoring functionality after the conflict. This painful process could lead to temporary economic losses for some, downsizing and divestments, and dilution of power or control over resources. The second tenet is building capacity to prevent or minimize future conflict. The third tenet is a positive transformation that calls for Sudan to shed its old self—characterized by selfishness and greed—in favor of a new Sudan governed by the ethos of Sudanism. The fourth tenet is adaptability, which I define as an evolutionary process designed to sustain peace and stability in the face of disruption and change. The AGNP must be decisive in leading this process.

- *Develop Reliable Social Infrastructure*

The destruction caused by the civil war in Sudan is extensive, affecting various sectors such as transportation, communication, energy, healthcare, education, and more. Rebuilding the infrastructure is, therefore, an arduous and complex task that requires careful planning, coordination, and investment. To that effect, the AGNP must develop a comprehensive plan outlining short-term and long-term goals for rebuilding the country's infrastructure.

A critical priority focus area of the AGNP's post-conflict reconstruction is the provision of essential facilities and services. These include hospitals, schools, water supply systems, and power grids. Restoration and enhancement of communication systems are vital, as these play a role in coordinating economic development efforts and connecting communities.[166] These services are critical for the wellbeing and stability of the population.

The reconstruction of essential facilities must be community-based. The AGNP must develop mechanisms for local communities' involvement in planning and decision-making.[167] Their input and participation are essential for the success and sustainability of the infrastructure rebuilding projects. Where need be, the AGNP should invest in training and capacity-building programs to equip local professionals with the skills needed to maintain and manage the rebuilt infrastructure effectively.[168]

Balanced regional development in post-conflict Sudan is essential to promote stability, reduce inequalities, and foster national unity. It involves ensuring that economic growth, infrastructure development, and public services are distributed equitably across different regions of the country. The AGNP must devise a plan to address disparities and create opportunities for growth in underdeveloped regions. For instance, the AGNP could prioritize infrastructure development in regions that have been neglected heretofore. One way to accelerate this is to incentivize private investment in such regions. This could include tax breaks, grants, or subsidies to encourage businesses to operate in these areas.

Decentralizing government functions is also vital to empower local authorities and enable them to address regional issues more effectively. This includes considering an area's unique needs and devoting appropriate resources to each region, ensuring they are allocated fairly and transparently. The AGNP must develop accountability systems in allocating resources and implementing development projects to build trust and confidence among the population. A balanced regional development requires a long-term commitment from the AGNP and the active participation of all stakeholders.

Long-Term Recovery Actions

Long-term actions include transforming the education system, changing the country's name, relocating the capital city, abolishing tribalism, and reintegrating Sudan with South Sudan. These action points are discussed next.

- *Transform the Education System*

Education plays a vital role in shaping future generations' values, attitudes, and beliefs. It is pivotal in rebuilding a nation and fostering social cohesion. Education can contribute significantly to the healing and rebuilding of a fractured Sudan by nurturing a sense of shared identity and mutual respect.[169] Transforming the education system of post-conflict Sudan is undoubtedly an uphill battle but also an indispensable task.

Over the years, Sudan's education system has undergone several changes, and the outcomes have been described as devastating to the country's economy and the wellbeing of its citizens.[170] The last notable change was inspired by an ideological agenda in which the main goal was to remold the Sudanese identity around political Islam, with education used as the tool for identity change toward character-building and personal development.[171] As noble as the ideology sounded, the more root-bound national ethos that would unify people remained elusive.

Peace in Sudan offers the established AGNP another chance to look at the current state of the education system, identify the gaps, and understand the population's specific needs. A clear and comprehensive educational vision that aligns with our philosophy of Sudanism is imperative.

As the AGNP embarks on rebuilding educational facilities destroyed during the conflict, there is a need to review the existing curriculum to ensure it is relevant and inclusive and promotes critical thinking, tolerance, and peacebuilding. This requires a collective effort from the government, civil society, and Sudan partners to build a resilient system that contributes to lasting peace and development in the country.

The reviewed education system should promote the use of national symbols and celebrations that represent the unity and diversity of the people. It should emphasize the shared values and identity that bind the Sudanese together. The process must involve local communities in the education system by inviting parents, community leaders, and representatives from diverse backgrounds to participate in decision-making. This inclusivity can generate a sense of ownership and unity in education.

- *Change Country Name and Relocate Capital City*

What about changing the capital? In fact, why not change the name of Sudan? This might seem a wild thought on the face of it, but, thinking critically, it may well be a welcome idea for some. As mentioned earlier, divorcing from 67 years of repeated failure requires radical thinking and revolutionary actions. Changing the name of Sudan and relocating the capital city may represent a psychological break from the stereotypes of failure associated with the old names and locations.

Following the fighting between SAF and RSF, some of those who fled the fighting in Khartoum hold memories that may never be forgotten in their lifetime. They lost everything: property, savings, family members, and memories. Some may never want to come back to Khartoum. For them, it would be a relief to wake up to a new home divorced from the turbulent past.

During the last 30 years, Sudan was associated with a negative reputation and became isolated and unmentioned, even in weather forecasts. Changing the country's name could be one of the ways to present a fresh face to the world. Obviously, this will change nothing without a shift from the old ways of doing things. Nevertheless, it could present a positive perception to the Sudanese and the world.

There could also be an objective reason for changing the name from Sudan to a more inclusive and representative name. A likely inclusive name could be one that bears the significance of the people, the land, the cultures, and the history. Does "Sudan" represent all these elements? Something to consider. I have no specific preference here but will provide pointers to enrich this debate.

Changing a country's name is not out of the norm. Many countries changed names as part of transiting into nation-states or as a sign of breaking away from a turbulent past. Some countries retained the original name with minor changes, while others moved fundamentally into new names. For instance, Burma changed to Myanmar, Swaziland changed to Eswatini, the Great Socialist People's Libyan Arab Jamahiriya became simply Libya, Zaire changed to the Democratic Republic of the Congo, Rhodesia became Zimbabwe, Dahomey changed to Benin, Bechuanaland became Botswana, Gold Coast changed its name to Ghana, Upper Volta became Burkina Faso, and Nyasaland changed to Malawi.

Other countries split up names, changed naming structures, or removed parts of their names. Most former Soviet Union member countries and former constituents of Czechoslovakia changed their names following a split from the Union. The motivation for name changes differs from nation to nation, but the common denominator is that countries change names as a symbol of what will hopefully be a more promising, inclusive, and representative future. The point is that a name change often accompanies fundamental political changes but, in most cases, confers an overwhelming national desire to break from the painful past and move into a brighter future.[172]

Moving Nigeria's capital from Lagos to Abuja was a significant event in the country's history. The decision to move the capital was made to address several challenges associated with Lagos being the capital city and to promote national unity and development. By having the capital in a more central location, the government aimed to reduce regional imbalances and promote a sense of inclusivity among the various ethnic and cultural groups in the country. By moving the capital away from Lagos—the country's economic center—the government sought to decentralize power and foster the development of other regions.[173]

Sudan, too, can adapt by relocating its capital from Khartoum to a more sociopolitical and economically strategic region. On this front, I am aware that relocating the capital city of a country emerging from civil war is a complex and momentous decision that can have profound implications for the nation's stability, development, and unity.

Engaging with the public, key stakeholders, and communities is essential to gain support and ensure social cohesion during the transition.

If the Sudanese decide to relocate the capital, viable options could include Wad Medani, El-Obeid, Merowe, Port-Sudan, Dongola, Kassala, or Nyala, to name just a few. All those cities have strategic locations, vast lands, and economic activity centers. However, if Khartoum is to be retained as capital, efforts should be undertaken to decentralize services and economic activities to make the city less congested.

A less radical solution is to adopt the South African style of having multiple capitals. Sudan could develop a commercial capital, an industrial capital, an administrative capital, and a cultural capital. Services would be decentralized, and development could proliferate equitably. Khartoum holds a quarter of Sudan's population, while its landmass is less than 1 percent of the country. This represents a deformity beyond proportions. Had Khartoum been smaller and less strategic, the limited war between SAF and RSF would not have resulted in such damage to the country.

A capital city symbolizes a country's sovereignty and is built strategically for peace and war resilience. There are great lessons to be learned from Kyiv in how it has endured attacks with the most sophisticated and highly destructive weapons during the Russia-Ukraine war.[174] Ukraine built Kyiv to withstand war and destruction. Kyiv is well-prepared with underground fireproof bunkers, reserve power and water supplies, and underground stocks of food and medical supplies.[175] Not only that, but Ukraine also owns multiple alternative urban centers ready to replace Kyiv as capital should Kyiv be incapacitated. [174]

The Swedish Royal Airforce developed and adopted decentralized operationalization and deployment of its core military assets, including aircraft, by building airbases in remote and inaccessible locations.[176] Ukraine adopted the Swedish model and insulated its military assets from destruction to a large extent. In contrast, the destruction of Khartoum in the contemporary scheme of events means the destruction of Sudan. War is never a remote possibility. Large cities can sometimes be taken as military targets to push an adversary to surrender. This is comparable to how the United States forced Japan's capitulation by dropping nuclear bombs on Hiroshima and Nagasaki.

Should Sudan go to war with another country in the future, and should Khartoum be taken out in multiple airstrikes, Sudan will have no option but to surrender. Even in the case of the limited internal war between SAF and RSF, it was clear that no other city in Sudan had the infrastructure to accommodate those who fled Khartoum. Some of those who fled to other locations within Sudan decided to return to the capital even as they faced the risk of losing their lives simply because of the challenges they faced in their relocation stations. That said, intellectuals are invited to debate a new name for Sudan and the new capital city, which will be subjected to a referendum at the end.

■ *Abolish Tribalism for Good*

Tribal or ethnic origin represents a source of pride since identifying with ethnicity fosters belonging and protection. However, it should not be at the expense of allegiance to the nation-state, nor should it be used as a tool for discriminating against or scorning other ethnic groups. Sudanese hold pride in their ethnic and tribal origins. Most modern nations were built originally from fragmented social and ethnic clusters, wherein nation-building gradually shifted tribal allegiance to nationhood commitment. This was a painful and lengthy process, and some countries had to use military might to unify nations.

On the negative side, tribalism is the favoritism and prioritization of the interest of one's cultural group at the expense of the greater good of everyone.[177] Without oversimplification, tribalism is frequently at the heart of most civil wars.[178] It is probably the worst manifestation of corruption at the heart of most if not all, civil conflicts in Africa.[179] Stamping out tribalism should be the number one agenda of Sudan's post-conflict reconstruction. When leaders lead by good example, they ensure that their followers take the cue, irrespective of who the leaders are or for how long or short they are in power.

I mentioned examples from across Africa that illustrate this idea in this book. A classic example is Tanzania under the leadership of then-president Mwalimu Julius Kambarage Nyerere, an unwavering believer in the unity of African nations and an icon of leadership with integrity and commitment. Nyerere advanced the novel political ideology of Ujamaa. He envisioned an equitable society where resources and benefits were shared with all Tanzanians as a people. This philosophy fostered a sense of patriotism and pride in the Tanzanian heritage.

While implementing the Ujamaa model faced enormous logical and sustainability challenges in the face of growing economic difficulties, the philosophy was pivotal to the political stability and social cohesion that Tanzania has enjoyed since independence and continues to enjoy today. Tanzania remains one of the few African countries to have hardly experienced any of the civil wars and political instability that have characterized nearly all its neighbors.[180]

Abolishing tribalism is a process, not an event—meaning that time must be invested. Most importantly, it is a collective effort involving multiple actors at various levels. In Chapter Four, I introduced the concept of Sudanism. Like Tanzania's Ujamaa philosophy, Sudanism envisions a unified Sudanese identity transcending tribal or cultural divisions. This must be the immediate rallying call of the AGNP in their deeds and actions. The AGNP must make a declaration that emphasizes equality, mutual respect, and commitment to ending tribalism and cultural discrimination.

The principle of Sudanese identity must override tribal identity. First, this must be reflected in the AGNP's composition to ensure that critical administrative appointments are not dominated by ethnicity or cultural background to forestall nepotism. Second, post-conflict reconstruction and development must be evenly distributed across the nation, and regional imbalances must be corrected through affirmative action.[166] Sudan has the requisite elements to elevate from tribal allegiances to a nation-state.

Policymakers and intellectuals should preach for the union and desist from promoting policies, cultures, and practices that promote the spirit of tribalism. Abolishing tribalism is not a process that will end soon, but it must begin and be premised on policies and procedures that gradually transition people's fidelities from ethnic group to nation.

Eventually, a society-wide movement will gain momentum when people see the value of unifying around a national agenda rather than tribal domes.

One must note that Sudanism does not contradict changing the country's name. Sudanism is a philosophy that can bear any name. If Sudan changed its name, then Sudanism would be adapted to the new name. The principle does not even have to rhyme with the country name. For instance, Ujama, Harambee, and Ubuntu are not derived from country names but are taken based on their cultural or historical significance.

- *Reintegrate the Two Sudans*

While it may sound remote or unrealistic at face value, Sudan can also pursue the ambitious goal of reintegrating with South Sudan. The reintegration process refers to the coming together of Sudan and South Sudan as territories that were once part of a single country. Reintegration can be complex and sensitive, often involving political negotiations, addressing historical grievances, and the people's will.

One of the most notable examples of successful reintegration is the reunification of East and West Germany. Following World War II, Germany was divided into two countries with different political systems: East Germany and West Germany.[181] In 1990, after the fall of the Berlin Wall and the end of the Cold War, the two German states were reunified into a single nation, the Federal Republic of Germany.[182] The successful reunification of Germany was attributed to strong public support among the Germans. The desire for reunification was a significant driving force that united the population and overcame some integration challenges.

The reintegrated Sudan must make a solid commitment to peace and reconciliation. The AGNP must emphasize its dedication to being a responsible member of the international community and working toward peace and stability in Africa and beyond. It must engage in extensive diplomatic efforts to strengthen relations with neighboring countries and other key partners. Without being overly zealous about the reintegration of the two Sudans, and while faithfully praying that I will celebrate it in my lifetime, I believe there could be a myriad of possibilities for the two-countries-one-nation to reintegrate around economic interests.

For instance, economic integration, single currency, visa-less entry, and integrative mega infrastructure projects could benefit both countries. This requires visionary political leaders on both sides who can see the bigger picture, rise above ideological and political interests, and put the wellbeing of their nations above any other consideration. In chapter one of this book, I mentioned some ingredients to make such an integration successful. Such a project would undoubtedly be celebrated by the citizens of the two countries owing to the culture and history they have in common. It remains a question of political will to make this a reality.

The two countries can benefit from several examples from within Africa and beyond. I have great friends from Sudan and South Sudan; some are policymakers, senior executives, and political activists. We discuss some of these issues in our social media groups, and I know their sentiment and desires for a long-term form of togetherness. I, therefore, do not doubt that the idea of north-south or south-north togetherness will be welcome. Africa is moving toward integration, and I firmly hold that Sudan and South Sudan could find a form of integration that does not necessarily result in the loss of sovereignty of either.

Those who have monitored Sudan-related politics closely may have observed the extent to which conflicting parties in South Sudan were more prepared to accept north Sudan mediation during the peace negotiations between Salva Kiir and Riek Machar. Likewise, South Sudan played a pivotal role in the Juba accord that paved the way for a transitional government after the 2019 revolution. There is a form of positive chemistry that still exists despite historic grievances. It is a sense of concealed love and a feeling of having a big brother that pushes Khartoum to go to Juba and pushes Juba to come to Khartoum to seek advice and support when in trouble. This positive chemistry will play a pivotal role in accomplishing a potential togetherness in the future.

Conclusion

For 67 years, Sudan has been under self-rule with little achievement for its people to be proud of.

For 67 years, the Sudanese people have not agreed on a system of governance, a consensual constitution, power alternation principles, peaceful cohabitation, or an equitable development model.

Sixty-seven years and the Sudanese are among the poorest nations on Earth while sitting on abundant and coveted resources—ecological diversity, land vastness, water abundance, mineral resources, cultural heritage, intelligent people, ideal geopolitical location, and fertile land.

Sixty-seven years and the Sudanese have failed to live in peace together, with nearly all wars fought internally while parts of the country are under occupation by other nations.

Sixty-seven years and the Sudanese are packing for a mass exodus from their own country to find a better life in countries that erstwhile looked up to them for technical expertise and knowledge transfer.

Sixty-seven years, Sudan failed to build reliable social infrastructure, improve people's living standards, secure necessities, or provide social welfare.

Albert Einstein once said: "Insanity is doing the same thing over and over again and expecting different results."[183] Likewise, if Sudan has failed to elevate its status after 67 years of doing the same thing over and over, it ought to radically change its way of doing things, return to the drawing board, format its memory of past storage, and upload fresh ideas. Formatting the memory and uploading fresh ideas require revolutionary thinking, radical actions, and irreversible divorce from nostalgia to beliefs or actions held historically to be true.

In this book, I have attempted to throw a stone into a lake that has been stagnant for decades. I have orthodoxically adopted this approach of outside-the-box thinking. Some may find these ideas wild or unrealistic. However, those who concur that Sudan needs a fresh jumpstart will agree with my thoughts in this book.

The ideas I presented in this book, particularly those related to the change of the country's name, relocation of the capital city, abolition of tribalism, merging of several ministries into one, relocation of army barracks outside populated areas, and resetting of the education system, among others, are in line with this mode of thinking.

To build a resilient nation, Sudan must foster a Sudanism identity that offers a place under the sun for each of its bearers, irrespective of their cultural, religious, political, or social background.

To build foundations for a solid economy, Sudan must consolidate efforts to exploit its natural resources, invest in education, and prioritize the establishment of a decentralized system of resource governance.

To achieve sustainable peace, Sudanese must agree on how the country should be ruled rather than focusing on which ethnic group should rule.

To build a proud nation, Sudanese must recognize that no culture is superior to another culture and, as such, all cultures must be given equal weight and opportunity to be preserved and promoted.

To preserve unity, religion should not be confounded with politics. As such, religion should be made an element of strength and unity, not an element of social segregation. I lived in Kenya—a faithfully Christian country—for over 15 years, and I have never been subjected to any form of discrimination because I am a Muslim. In fact, I studied for my PhD at a Christian university, and I have never been denied any right, including the right to practice my faith undisturbed.

Based on a conviction that transforming Sudan requires courageous steps and practical ideas, I have proposed a 12-point plan that can be adapted to transition the country from regression to *progression*. Each of the 12 action points includes several sub-action points and requires specific resource types. These actions are reported in detail in Appendix One.

I have proposed an AGNP comprising eight service portfolios to implement an urgent transition program up to the national elections. To break the tendency of perceiving ministerial positions as a form of financial reward or an upgraded social status, I recommend adopting the names "first officer" for the prime minister, "second officer" for the deputy prime minister, and "secretary" for the cabinet ministers. This is because "secretary" and "officer" connote the sense of being in the service of people and are aligned with the notions of the servant leader.

The AGNP will comprise the positions of first officer (prime minister); second officer (deputy prime minister); secretary of regular forces and homeland; secretary for economy, finance, and national planning; secretary for national education, training, and capacity development; secretary for justice, peace, and social cohesion; secretary for health; and secretary for infrastructure and natural resources in addition to the governor of the central bank. The central bank should be renamed "National Bank of Sudan" to foster a nationalist rather than centric drive.

Each cabinet portfolio will be assigned time-sensitive deliverables. Every secretary is accountable to the first officer and the second officer. Every appointed secretary will sign performance contracts subject to periodic review for the duration of the transition. The unsatisfactory performance will trigger the annulation of the assignment. The performance contracts will be prepared by local consultants who will also be assisting the first officer in the performance review process. The agile government proposal is provided in Appendix Two.

These propositions are neither conclusive nor exclusive and are subject to alteration considering unfolding realities. They can be adjusted based on objective assessment and emergent situations. Nonetheless, they constitute a starting point for a nationwide debate. Sudan must begin somewhere but with fresh thinking.

I am not a politician and have never participated in any active political program or party. Therefore, my thoughts are not subject to any form of influence or contaminated by political allegiance. If some political affiliations do not agree with the thoughts I put forth in this book, it is already a positive sign that the thoughts I have provided will not reproduce the same historic failure. Instead, they should contribute to *stoning the Devil of war in Sudan.*

REFERENCES

1   **Associated Press**. *United Nations Humanitarian Chief says Sudan appears to be in a civil war "of the most brutal kind"*, Associated Press. Cited July 10, 2023. https://www.usnews.com/news/world/articles/2023-07-10/united-nations-humanitarian-chief-says-sudan-appears-to-be-in-a-civil-war-of-the-most-brutal-kind

2   **McCallum, D.** 2009. *Satan and his Kingdom: What the Bible says and how it matters to you.* Bethany House.

3   **Laughlin, V.A.** 2015. A Brief overview of al jinn within Islamic cosmology and religiosity. *Journal of Adventist Mission Studies,* 11(1): 067-078. https://doi.org/10.32597/jams/vol11/iss1/9/

4   **Kelly, H.A.** 2006. *Satan: A biography.* Cambridge University Press.

5   **Dieste, J.L.M.** 2013. 5. Among the jnûn: Possessions, magic and psychosomatic afflictions. In: *Health and Ritual in Morocco,* pp. 211-272. Brill.

6   **Mans, U.** 2004. Briefing: Sudan: the new war in Darfur. *African Affairs,* 103(411): 291-294. https://doi.org/10.1093/afraf/adh047

7   **Collins, R.O.** 2008. *A history of modern Sudan.* Cambridge University Press

8   **Poggo, S.S.** 2002. General Ibrahim Abboud's military administration in the Sudan, 1958-1964: Implementation of the programs of Islamization and Arabization in the Southern Sudan. *Northeast African Studies,* 9(1): 67-101. https://doi.org/10.1353/nas.2007.0002

9   **Malwal, B.** 1990. The agony of the Sudan. *J. Democracy,* 1: 75-86. https://doi.org/10.1353/jod.1990.0024

10 **Fluehr-Lobban, C. & Lobban, R.** 2001. The Sudan since 1989: National Islamic Front rule. *Arab Studies Quarterly*: 1-9. https://www.jstor.org/stable/41858370

11 **Murphy, T.** 2021. Sudan's transition in the balance. *IAI Papers,* 21: 38. https://www.cespi.it/sites/default/files/osservatori/allegati/iaip2138.pdf

12 **Idris, K. & Yongdi, S.** 2004. Khartoum. Conference presentation at AAPG International Conference: October 24-27, 2004. Cancun, Mexico.

13 **Dobon, B., Hassan, H.Y., Laayouni, H., Luisi, P., Ricaño-Ponce, I., Zhernakova, A., Wijmenga, C., Tahir, H., Comas, D. & Netea, M.G.** 2015. The genetics of East African populations: a Nilo-Saharan component in the African genetic landscape. *Scientific Reports,* 5(1): 1-11. https://doi.org/10.1038/srep09996

14 **Vertin, Z.** 2019. Red Sea rivalries: The Gulf, the Horn, and the new geopolitics of the Red Sea. https://www.brookings.edu/articles/red-sea-rivalries-the-gulf-the-horn-and-the-new-geopolitics-of-the-red-sea/

15 **Gebregziabher, M., Amdeselassie, F., Esayas, R., Abebe, Z., Silvia, H., Teklehaimanot, A.A., Korte, J.E., Pearce, J.L. & Cochran, J.J.** 2022. Geographical distribution of the health crisis of war in the Tigray region of Ethiopia. *Global Health,* 7(4): e008475. https://doi.org/10.1136/bmjgh-2022-008475

16 **Abdelfattah, M.A.** 2021. Climate change impact on water resources and food security in Egypt and possible adaptive measures. *Emerging Challenges to Food Production and Security in Asia, Middle East, and Africa: Climate Risks and Resource Scarcity*: 267-291. https://doi.org/10.1007/978-3-030-72987-5_10

17 **Gebresenbet, F. & Wondemagegnehu, D.Y.** 2021. New dimensions in the Grand Ethiopian Renaissance Dam negotiations: Ontological security in Egypt and Ethiopia. *African Security,* 14(1): 80-106. https://doi.org/10.1080/19392206.2021.1905921

18   **Trapenberg Frick, K.** 2021. No permanent friends, no permanent enemies: Agonistic ethos, tactical coalitions, and sustainable infrastructure. *Journal of Planning Education and Research,* 41(1): 62-78. https://doi.org/10.1177/0739456X18773491

19   **Chanie, B.S.** 2021. Sudan and South Sudan: an unamicable political divorce. *Global Change, Peace & Security,* 33(1): 61-76. https://doi.org/10.1080/14781158.2021.1880384

20   **Jarad, A., Attwairi, A., Elaswed, T. & Elmghirbi, E.** 2022. The role of the southern Libyan Saharan cities in building their relations with neighbouring countries. *Glasnik Srpskog geografskog drustva,* 102(1): 141-156. https://doi.org/10.2298/GSGD2201141J

21   **Styan, D.** 2022. Djibouti bridging the Gulf of Aden?: Balancing ports, patronage and military bases between Yemen's war and the Horn. In: *The Gulf States and the Horn of Africa,* pp. 229-248. Manchester University Press.

22   **Eberhard-Ruiz, A. & Calabrese, L.** 2017. Would more trade facilitation lead to lower transport costs in the East African Community? Institution.

23   **Kraska, J. & Wilson, B.** 2009. Combating pirates of the Gulf of Aden: The Djibouti Code and the Somali Coast Guard. *Ocean & Coastal Management*: 1-5. https://doi.org/10.1016/j.ocecoaman.2009.07.002

24   **Mkutu, K.** 2023. The frontier on the doorstep: Development and conflict dynamics in the southern rangelands of Kenya. *Journal of Eastern African Studies*: 1-18. https://doi.org/10.1080/17531055.2023.2227938

25   **Brooks, D.H. & Menon, J.** 2008. *Infrastructure and trade in Asia.* Edward Elgar Publishing.

26   **Chaban, N., Elgstrom, O. & Holland, M.** 2006. European Union as others see it, The. *The European Foreign Affairs Review,* 11: 245. https://doi.org/10.54648/EERR2006019

27   **Fantessi, A.A. & Kiprop, S.K.** 2015. Financial development and economic growth in West African Economic and Monetary Union (WAEMU). *African Journal of Business Management,* 9(17): 624-632. https://doi.org/10.5897/AJBM2015.7861

28 **Adam, A.M., Kyei, K., Moyo, S., Gill, R. & Gyamfi, E.N.** 2022. Similarities in Southern African Development Community (SADC) exchange rate markets structure: evidence from the ensemble empirical mode decomposition. *Journal of African Business,* 23(2): 516-530. https://doi.org/10.1080/1522 8916.2021.1874795

29 **Ebaidalla, E.M. & Ali, M.E.M.** 2023. Assessing intra-Arab Trade integration and potential: Evidence from the stochastic frontier gravity model. *The International Trade Journal,* 37(2): 221-239. https://doi.org/10.1080/08853908.2022.2029725

30 **Mohamed, E.S.E.** 2020. Resource rents, human development and economic growth in Sudan. *Economies,* 8(4): 1-22. https://doi.org/10.3390/economies8040099

31 **Elbadawi, I. & Suliman, K.M.** 2018. The macroeconomics of the gold economy in Sudan. Conference presentation at The Economic Research Forum (ERF). https://erf.org.eg/app/uploads/2018/06/1203_Final.pdf

32 **Bouabdellah, M. & Slack, J.F.** 2016. *Mineral deposits of North Africa.* Springer.

33 **Hamad, O.E.-T. & El-Battahani, A.** 2005. Sudan and the Nile Basin. *Aquatic Sciences,* 67: 28-41. https://doi.org/10.1007/s00027-004-0767-9

34 **Abdalla, A.A. & Abdel Nour, H.** 2001. The agricultural potential of Sudan. *Executive Intelligence Review,* 28(8): 37-45. https://doi.org/10.1007/978-3-030-72987-5_10

35 **Elmqvist, B., Olsson, L., Mirghani Elamin, E. & Warren, A.** 2005. A traditional agroforestry system under threat: an analysis of the Gum Arabic market and cultivation in Sudan. *Agroforestry systems,* 64: 211-218. https://doi.org/10.1007/s10457-004-2371-3

36 **Knobelsdorf, V.** 2005. The Nile waters agreements: Imposition and impacts of a transboundary legal system. *Colum. J. Transnat'l L.,* 44: 1-29. https://www.jurisafrica.org/wp-content/uploads/2021/07/Nile-River-Agreement-by-Valerie-Knobelsdorf.pdf

37 **Ali, K.M.M.** 2021 Water resources assessment, sustainable long-term development and management strategy, West and Central Darfur States, Sudan. Alneelain University.

38 **Hassan, R., Hertzler, G. & Benhin, J.K.** 2009. Depletion of forest resources in Sudan: Intervention options for optimal control. *Energy Policy,* 37(4): 1195-1203. https://doi.org/10.1016/j.enpol.2008.10.049

39 **Collins, R.O.** 2005. *Civil wars and revolution in the Sudan: Essays on the Sudan, Southern Sudan and Darfur, 1962-2004.* Tsehai Publishers.

40 **Thomas, E.** 2015. *South Sudan: a slow liberation.* Bloomsbury Publishing.

41 **Bach, J.-N. & Deshayes, C.** 2021. Sudan. In: *Africa Yearbook Volume 17,* pp. 392-404. Brill.

42 **Yaakop, M.R., Eltom, E.-N., Seman, A., Taib, R., Zawaw, H.Y., Jazimin, N.S. & Dewi, S.A.A.** 2018. Political implications of natural resources conflict in Sudan. *International Journal of Academic Research in Business and Social Sciences,* 8(2): 134-148. https://doi.org/10.6007/IJARBSS/v8-i2/3862

43 **Osman, M.A., Onono, J.O., Olaka, L.A., Elhag, M.M. & Abdel-Rahman, E.M.** 2021. Climate variability and change affect crops yield under rainfed conditions: A case study in Gedaref State, Sudan. *Agronomy,* 11(9): 1-24. https://doi.org/10.3390/agronomy11091680

44 **Johnson, D.H.** 2011. *The root causes of Sudan's civil wars: Peace or truce.* Boydell & Brewer.

45 **Sharkey, H.J.** 2008. Arab identity and ideology in Sudan: The politics of language, ethnicity, and race. *African Affairs,* 107(426): 21-43. https://doi.org/10.1093/afraf/adm068

46 **Deng, L.A.** 2013. *The Power of creative reasoning: the ideas and vision of John Garang.* Iuniverse.

47 **Al-Ajamee, M., Mahmoud, M.M. & Ali, A.M.** 2022. Khartoum Geohazard: An assessment and a future warning. Conference presentation at Geohazard Mitigation: Select Proceedings of VCDRR 2021. Springer. https://doi.org/10.1007/978-981-16-6140-2_8

48 **Campbell, S.** 2000. The changing role and identity of capital cities in the global era. Conference presentation at Annual Meeting of the Association of American Geographers, Pittsburgh, PA. https://www-personal.umich.edu/~sdcamp/AAG2000.html

49 **Flower, H.I.** 2009. *Roman republics.* Princeton University Press.

50 **Worthen, H. & Worthen, H.** 2020. Martial's damnatio ad bestias. *Humanism, Drama, and Performance: Unwriting Theatre*: 63-97. https://doi.org/10.1007/978-3-030-44066-4_2

51 **Azam, J.-P.** 2002. Looting and conflict between ethnoregional groups: Lessons for state formation in Africa. *Journal of Conflict Resolution,* 46(1): 131-153. https://doi.org/10.1177/0022002702046001008

52 **Hassan, M. & Kodouda, A.** 2023. Dismantling old or forging new clientelistic ties? Sudan's civil service reform after uprising. *World Development,* 169: 106232. https://doi.org/10.1016/j.worlddev.2023.106232

53 **Desta, Y.** 2019. Manifestations and causes of civil service corruption in developing countries. *Journal of Public Administration and Governance,* 9(3): 23-35. https://doi.org/10.5296/jpag.v9i3.14930

54 **Gal, R.** 1985. Commitment and obedience in the military: An Israeli case study. *Armed Forces & Society,* 11(4): 553-564. https://doi.org/10.1177/0095327X8501100405

55 **Kasher, A.** 2002. Between obedience and discipline: between law and ethics. *Professional Ethics, A Multidisciplinary Journal,* 10(2/3/4): 97-122. https://doi.org/10.5840/profethics2002102/3/416

56 **Oxford Analytica** 2021. Sudan Jihadist claims will stoke concerns. *Emerald Expert Briefings.* https://doi.org/10.1108/OXAN-ES264453

57 **Peksen, D.** 2009. Better or worse? The effect of economic sanctions on human rights. *Journal of Peace Research,* 46(1): 59-77. https://doi.org/10.1177/0022343308098404

58 **Omer, A.S., Bezruchka, S., Longhi, D., Kelly, Z., Brown, M. & Hagopian, A.** 2014. The effects of household assets inequality

and conflict on population health in Sudan. *African Population Studies,* 28(3): 1216-1232. https://doi.org/10.11564/0-0-611

59 **Hassan, K. & Abdullah, A.** 2015. Effect of oil revenue and the Sudan economy: Econometric model for services sector GDP. *Procedia-Social and Behavioral Sciences,* 172: 223-229. https://doi.org/10.1016/j.sbspro.2015.01.358

60 **Chang, Y.-H. & Liao, M.-Y.** 2009. The effect of aviation safety education on passenger cabin safety awareness. *Safety Sciences,* 47(10): 1337-1345. https://doi.org/10.1016/j.ssci.2009.02.001

61 **Warburg, G.** 2011. Sudan during the Mahdist State. *Middle Eastern Studies,* 47(4): 675-682. https://doi.org/10.1080/00263 206.2011.589969

62 **Rungta, R.** 1966. Sudan transport: A history of railway, marine, and river services in the Republic of Sudan. *Business History Review,* 40(3): 394-395. https://doi.org/10.2307/3112454

63 **Christopher, A.** 2008 A case study on Kenya Airways. Kenya. Multimedia University. Unpublished Doctorate Dissertation

64 **Fetais, A.H.M., Al-Kwifi, O.S., Ahmed, Z.U. & Tran, D.K.** 2020. Qatar Airways: Building a global brand. *Journal of Economic and Administrative Sciences,* 37(3): 319-336. https://doi.org/10.1108/JEAS-04-2020-0044

65 **Meichsner, N.A., O'Connell, J.F. & Warnock-Smith, D.** 2018. The future for African air transport: Learning from Ethiopian Airlines. *Journal of transport geography,* 71: 182-197. https://doi.org/10.1016/j.jtrangeo.2018.06.020

66 **De Waal, A.** 2015. *The real politics of the Horn of Africa: Money, war and the business of power.* John Wiley & Sons.

67 **Imam, Z.A.** 2013 Search for transitional justice in Darfur: the role of the traditional mechanisms.

68 **Arnold, M. & LeRiche, M.** 2013. *South Sudan: From revolution to independence.* Oxford University Press, USA.

69 **Reynolds, M.T.** 2010. Legitimizing the ICC: Supporting the court's prosecution of those responsible in Darfur. *Boston College Third World Law Journal,* 30: 179. https://lira.bc.edu/work/ns/c8837092-2c9c-4ba1-a1d5-8f032447f1a8

70 **Johnson, D.H.** 2003. *The root causes of Sudan's civil wars.* Indiana University Press.

71 **Betts, W.S., Carlson, S.N. & Gisvold, G.** 2000. The post-conflict transitional administration of Kosovo and the lessons learned in efforts to establish a judiciary and the rule of Law. *Mich. J. Int'l L.,* 22: 371. https://repository.law.umich.edu/cgi/viewcontent.cgi?article=1375&context=mjil

72 **Agwanda, B. & Asal, U.Y.** 2020. State fragility and post-conflict state-building: An analysis of South Sudan Conflict (2013-2019). *Güvenlik Bilimleri Dergisi,* 9(1): 125-146. https://doi.org/10.28956/gbd.736103

73 **Weiss, R.** 2020. Peacebuilding, democratization, and political reconciliation in Cambodia. *Asian Journal of Peacebuilding,* 8(1): 113-131. https://doi.org/10.18588/202005.00a069

74 **Linabary, J.R., Krishna, A. & Connaughton, S.L.** 2017. The Conflict Family: Storytelling as an Activity and a Method for Locally Led, Community-Based Peacebuilding. *Conflict Resolution Quarterly,* 34(4): 431-453. https://doi.org/10.1002/crq.21189

75 **Falaschetti, D.** 2009. *Democratic governance and economic performance: how accountability can go too far in politics, law, and business.* Vol. 14. Springer Science & Business Media.

76 **Rhodes, R.A.W. & Hart, P.t.** 2014. *The Oxford handbook of political leadership.* Oxford Handbooks.

77 **Deng, F.** 2018. *The challenges of fragile states: Conflict and cooperation in the Horn of Africa.* Palgrave Macmillan.

78 **Jentzsch, C., Kalyvas, S.N. & Schubiger, L.I.** 2015. Militias in civil wars. *Journal of Conflict Resolution,* 59(5): 755-769. https://doi.org/10.1177/0022002715576753

79 **Hazen, J.** 2005. Social integration of ex-combatants after civil war. Conference presentation at United Nations expert group meeting entitled "Dialogue in the Social Integration Process: Building Peaceful Social Relations—By, For, and With People. https://www.un.org/esa/socdev/sib/egm/paper/Jennifer%20Hazen.pdf

80 **Newman, E. & Schnabel, A.** 2002. *Recovering from civil conflict: reconciliation, peace, and development.* Vol. 11. Psychology Press.

81 **Adeagbo, O.A. & Iyi, J.-M.** 2011. Post-election crisis in Kenya and internally displaced persons: a critical appraisal. *J. Pol. & L.,* 4: 174. https://doi.org/doi.org/10.5539/jpl.v4n2p174

82 **Suto, J.M.** 2014 Reconciliation in divided societies: A case study of the Kenyan Truth, Justice, and Reconciliation Commission. University of Nairobi.

83 **Materu, S.F.** 2014. *The post-election violence in Kenya: Domestic and international legal responses.* Vol. 2. Springer.

84 **Shaka, J.** 2016. Beyond Violence: Transitional Justice in Kenya. *Available at SSRN 2797689.* https://doi.org/10.2139/ssrn.2797689

85 **Jensen, S., Kelly, T., Andersen, M.K., Christiansen, C. & Sharma, J.R.** 2017. Torture and ill-treatment under perceived: human rights documentation and the poor. *Human Rights Quarterly,* 39: 393. https://doi.org/10.1353/hrq.2017.0023

86 **Rose, M.M.** 2017. Bound by conflict: Dilemmas of the two Sudans. *Journal for Peace and Justice Studies,* 27(2): 127-129. https://doi.org/10.5840/peacejustice201727218

87 **Carolan, G.** 2021. Statebuilding in the peace agreements of Sudan and South Sudan. *Journal of Intervention and Statebuilding,* 15(1): 1-24. https://doi.org/10.1080/17502977.2019.1703492

88 **Johnson, D.H.** 2016. *South Sudan: A new history for a new nation.* Ohio University Press.

89 **Garang, K.** 2019. Political Ideology and organisational espousal: A political-historical analysis of Dr. John Garang De Mabior's "New Sudan Vision". *Modern Africa: Politics, History and Society,* 7(2): 89-122. https://doi.org/10.26806/modafr.v7i2.258

90 **Gibia, R.** 2005. *Where is our sudanism* Sudan Tribune, Cited July 9, 2023. https://sudantribune.com/article26857

91 **Kimambo, I.N. & Maddox, G.H.** 2019. *A New History of Tanzania.* Mkuki na Nyota Publishers.

92 **Otunnu, O.** 2015. Mwalimu Julius Kambarage Nyerere's philosophy, contribution, and legacies. *African Identities,* 13(1): 18-33. https://doi.org/10.1080/14725843.2014.961278

93 **Maliyamkono, T., Dimoso, P. & Mason, H.** 2022. Continuity with vision: The roadmap to success for President Samia Suluhu Hassan. TEMA & SIYAYA.

94 **Vershinina, N., Woldesenbet Beta, K. & Murithi, W.** 2018. How does national culture enable or constrain entrepreneurship? Exploring the role of Harambee in Kenya. *Journal of Small Business and Enterprise Development,* 25(4): 687-704. https://doi.org/10.1108/JSBED-03-2017-0143

95 **Onditi, F.** 2018. African national anthems: Their value system and normative potential. *African study monographs. Supplementary issue.,* 56(3): 3-20. https://doi.org/10.14989/230171

96 **Clark, P. & Kaufman, Z.D.** 2009. *After genocide: Transitional justice, post-conflict reconstruction and reconciliation in Rwanda and beyond.* Columbia University Press.

97 **Nabudere, D.W.** 2005. Ubuntu philosophy: memory and reconciliation. *Texas Scholar Works*: 1-20. http://hdl.handle.net/2152/4521

98 **Kamwangamalu, N.M.** 1999. Ubuntu in South Africa: A sociolinguistic perspective to a pan-African concept. *Critical arts,* 13(2): 24-41. https://doi.org/10.1080/02560049985310111

99 **Akinola, A.O. & Uzodike, U.O.** 2018. Ubuntu and the quest for conflict resolution in Africa. *Journal of Black Studies,* 49(2): 91-113. https://doi.org/10.1177/0021934717736186

100 **Tutu, D.M.** 2002. Attributes of leadership: words from leaders. *Verbum et Ecclesia,* 23(3): 621-624. https://doi.org/10.4102/ve.v23i3.1238

101 **Nolte, A. & Downing, C.** 2019. Ubuntu—the essence of caring and being: A concept analysis. *Holistic nursing practice,* 33(1): 9-16. https://doi.org/10.1097/HNP.0000000000000302

102 **Clark, P.** 2010. *The Gacaca courts, post-genocide justice and reconciliation in Rwanda: Justice without lawyers.* Cambridge University Press.

103 **Trompenaars, F. & Voerman, E.** 2010. *Servant leadership across cultures: Harnessing the strength of the world's most powerful leadership philosophy.* NY, McGraw Hill.

104 **National Anthems**. n.d. *Sudan National anthem,* Cited 11 July 2023. https://nationalanthems.info/sd.htm

105 **Bøås, M. & Dunn, K.C.** 2007. *African Guerrillas: raging against the machine.* Lynne Rienner Boulder, CO.

106 **Verwimp, P.** 2004. Death and survival during the 1994 genocide in Rwanda. *Population studies,* 58(2): 233-245. https://doi.org/10.1080/0032472042000224422

107 **Straus, S.** 2019. *The order of genocide: Race, power, and war in Rwanda.* Cornell University Press.

108 **Gourevitch, P. & Andrews, C.** 1999. We wish to inform you that tomorrow we will be killed with our families: stories from Rwanda. *Canadian Medical Association. Journal,* 160(4): 537. https://doi.org/10.1353/at.2000.0004

109 **Dallaire, R. & Sarty, R.** 2006. *Shake hands with the devil: the failure of humanity in Rwanda.* Canadian National Institute for the Blind.

110 **Finnström, S.** 2008. *Living with bad surroundings: War, history, and everyday moments in northern Uganda.* Duke University Press.

111 **Kirkby, C.** 2018. Rwanda's gacaca courts: A preliminary critique. *Journal of African Law,* 50(2): 94-117 https://www.jstor.org/stable/27607966

112 **Ramírez-Barat, C.** 2014. Transitional justice, culture, and society: Beyond outreach. *International Journal For Court Administration,* 6(2): 106-109. https://doi.org/10.18352/ijca.151

113 **Robinson, J.** 2017. *Transitional justice and the politics of inscription: Memory, space and narrative in Northern Ireland.* Routledge.

114 **Ingelaere, B.** 2016. *Inside Rwanda's Gacaca courts: Seeking justice after genocide.* University of Wisconsin Pres.

115 **Hatzfeld, J.** 2005. *Machete season: The killers in Rwanda speak.* Macmillan.

116 **Loyle, C.E.** 2018. Transitional justice and political order in Rwanda. *Ethnic and Racial Studies,* 41(4): 663-680. https://doi.org/10.1080/01419870.2017.1366537

117 **Schlight, J.** 1996. *A war too long: The USAF in Southeast Asia, 1961-1975.* Air Force History and Museums Program.

118 **Pearce, J.** 2012. Control, politics and identity in the Angolan civil war. *African Affairs,* 111(444): 442-465. https://doi.org/10.1093/afraf/ads028

119 **Vines, A.** 1999. *Angola Unravels: The rise and fall of the Lusaka peace process.* Vol. 3169. Human Rights Watch.

120 **Wolff, S.** 2011. Post-Conflict State Building: the debate on institutional choice. *Third World Quarterly,* 32(10): 1777-1802. https://doi.org/10.1080/01436597.2011.610574

121 **Moorman, M.** 2004. Angola: Anatomy of an oil State. JSTOR.

122 **Birmingham, D.** 2015. *A short history of modern Angola.* Oxford University Press.

123 **Zack-Williams, A.B.** 1999. Sierra Leone: The political economy of civil war, 1991-98. *Third World Quarterly,* 20(1): 143-162. https://doi.org/10.1080/01436599913965

124 **Tamm, I.J.** 2002. *Diamonds in peace and war: severing the conflict-diamond connection.* World Peace Foundation.

125 **Akhaze, R.E.** 2015 A comparative analysis of post-conflict peacebuilding in Liberia and Sierra Leone, 2000-2013. University of Lagos (Nigeria).

126 **Bellows, J. & Miguel, E.** 2009. War and local collective action in Sierra Leone. *Journal of public Economics,* 93(11-12): 1144-1157. https://doi.org/10.1016/j.jpubeco.2009.07.012

127 **Baker, B.** 2006. The African post-conflict policing agenda in Sierra Leone: Analysis. *Conflict, Security & Development,* 6(1): 25-49. https://doi.org/10.1080/14678800600590629

128 **Vines, A.** 1997. *Still killing: Landmines in Southern Africa. Human Rights Watch Arms Project.* https://www.hrw.org/reports/1997/lmsa/

129 **Lloyd, R.B.** 1995. Mozambique: The terror of war, the tensions of peace. *Current History,* 94(591): 152-155. https://doi.org/10.1525/curh.1995.94.591.152

130 **Kersten, M.** 2020. No justice without peace, but what peace is on offer? Palestine, Israel and the International Criminal Court. *Journal of International Criminal Justice,* 18(4): 1001-1015. https://doi.org/10.1093/jicj/mqaa050

131 **Hanlon, J.** 2003. *Peace without profit: How the IMF blocks rebuilding in Mozambique.* James Currey.

132 **Pitcher, M.A.** 2002. *Transforming Mozambique: the politics of privatization, 1975–2000.* Vol. 104. Cambridge University Press.

133 **Alden, C.** 2001. *Mozambique and the construction of the new African state.* Springer.

134 **Truth and Reconciliation Commission South Africa** 2002. *Truth and Reconciliation Commission of South Africa report.* Macmillan.

135 **Wilson, R.** 2001. *The politics of truth and reconciliation in South Africa: Legitimizing the post-apartheid state.* Cambridge University Press.

136 **Villa-Vicencio, C., Verwoerd, W., Rotberg, R.I. & Thompson, D.** 2003. Looking back reaching forward: Reflections on the Truth and Reconciliation Commission of South Africa. *Hypatia,* Hypatia (2): 189-196. https://philpapers.org/rec/VILLBR

137 **Del Castillo, G.** 2008. *Rebuilding war-torn states: The challenge of post-conflict economic reconstruction.* OUP Oxford.

138 **Hayner, P.B.** 2010. *Unspeakable Truths: Transitional justice and the challenge of truth commissions.* Routledge.

139 **Olsen, T.D., Payne, L.A. & Reiter, A.G.** 2010. *Transitional Justice in Balance: Comparing Processes.* Weighing Efficacy. Washington, United States Institute of Peace Press

140 **Barbour, K.M.** 1980. The Sudan since independence. *The Journal of Modern African Studies,* 18(1): 73-97. https://doi.org/10.1017/S0022278X00009459

141 **Foley, M.** 2013. *Political leadership: Themes, contexts, and critiques.* OUP UK.

142 **De Waal, A.** 1997. *Famine crimes: politics & the disaster relief industry in Africa.* Indiana University Press.

143 **O'Brien, R.J.** 2019 Models of spiritual leadership: Strategies for bridging the gap between policy and ethics. San José. San José State University. https://scholarworks.sjsu.edu/cgi/viewcontent.cgi?article=1035&context=etd_dissertations

144 **Ahmed, E.** 2022 Leadership strategy, resource orchestration, firm size, and organizational resilience among listed banks in Kenya. Nairobi, Kenya. Pan Africa Christian University. Unpublished Doctorate Dissertation.

145 **Brett, R. & Malagón, L.** 2022. Transitional justice and peace-making/peacebuilding. *Contemporary Peacemaking: Peace Processes, Peacebuilding and Conflict*: 475-505. https://doi.org/10.1007/978-3-030-82962-9_23

146 **Teitel, R.G.** 2000. *Transitional justice.* Oxford University Press, USA.

147 **Barahona de Brito, A.** 2010. Transitional justice and memory: Exploring perspectives. *South European Society and Politics,* 15(3): 359-376. https://doi.org/10.1080/13608746.2010.513599

148 **Shafiq, R.** 2015. *(In) justice and the experience of civilian survivors of armed conflict: Case studies from Palestine (Gaza), Iraq and Syria.* University of Surrey (United Kingdom).

149 **Ceva, E. & Murphy, C.** 2022. Interactive justice in transitional justice: A dynamic framework. *American Journal of Political Science,* 66(3): 762-774. https://doi.org/10.1111/ajps.12663

150 **Deng, F.M.** 2011. *War of visions: Conflict of identities in the Sudan.* Rowman & Littlefield.

151 **Heifetz, R.A.** 1994. *Leadership without easy answers.* Harvard University Press.

152 **Barnett, M. & Weiss, T.G.** 2018. *Humanitarianism in question: Politics, power, ethics.* Cornell University Press.

153 **Fast, L.** 2014. *Aid in danger: The perils and promise of humanitarianism.* University of Pennsylvania Press.

154 **Gberie, L.** 2005. *A dirty war in West Africa: The RUF and the destruction of Sierra Leone.* Indiana University Press.

155 **Clayton, G., Nathan, L. & Wiehler, C.** 2021. Ceasefire Success: A conceptual framework. *International Peacekeeping,*

28(3): 341-365. https://doi.org/10.1080/13533312.202 1.1894934

156 **Akebo, M.** 2016. *Ceasefire agreements and peace processes: A comparative study.* Taylor & Francis.

157 **Fisher, R., Ury, W.L. & Patton, B.** 2011. *Getting to yes: Negotiating agreement without giving in.* Penguin.

158 **Magone, C., Neuman, M. & Weissman, F.** 2012. *Humanitarian negotiations revealed: the MSF experience.* Oxford University Press.

159 **Williams, P.D.** 2016. *War and conflict in Africa.* John Wiley & Sons.

160 **Falola, T. & Njoku, R.C.** 2010. *War and peace in Africa.* North Carolina, Carolina Academic Press.

161 **Regehr, E.** 2015. *Disarming Conflict: Why Peace Cannot Be Won on the Battlefield.* Between the Lines.

162 **De Zeeuw, J.** 2007. *From soldiers to politicians: Transforming rebel movements after civil war.* Lynne Rienner Publishers.

163 **Hancock, L.E. & Mitchell, C.** 2018. *Local peacebuilding and legitimacy: interactions between national and local levels.* Routledge.

164 **Zwitter, A., Lamont, C.K., Heintze, H.-J. & Herman, J.** 2014. *Humanitarian action: global, regional and domestic legal responses.* Cambridge University Press.

165 **Kayes., D.C.** 2015. *Organizational Resilience. How Learning Sustains Organizations in Crisis, Disaster, and Breakdown.* New York, Oxford University Press.

166 **Coyne, C.J.** 2010. Rebuilding War-Torn States: The Challenge of Post-Conflict Economic Reconstruction, by Graciana Del Castillo. *Perspectives on Politics,* 8(1): 302-304. https://doi. org/10.1017/S153759270999288X

167 **Jackson, P.** 2020. Local government and decentralisation in post-conflict contexts. In: *Post-conflict Reconstruction and Local Government,* pp. 1-16. Routledge.

168 **Clément, M.J.A.** 2005. *Postconflict economics in Sub-Saharan Africa, lessons from the Democratic Republic of the Congo.* International Monetary Fund.

169 **Ghani, A. & Lockhart, C.** 2009. *Fixing failed states: A framework for rebuilding a fractured world.* Oxford University Press.

170 **Dafa'Alla, A.A., Hussein, E.S. & Adam, M.A.** 2016. Education in post-independence Sudan: a critical assessment. *International Journal of Sudan Research,* 6(1). https://doi.org/10.47556/J.IJSR.6.1.2016.3

171 **Gasim, G.** 2010. Reflecting on Sudan's higher education revolution under Al-Bashir's regime. *Journal of Comparative & International Higher Education,* 2(Fall): 50-53. https://www.ojed.org/index.php/jcihe/article/view/801

172 **Wanjiru, E.** 2006. Branding African countries: A prospect for the future. *Place Branding,* 2(1): 84-95. https://doi.org/10.1057/palgrave.pb.5990047

173 **Falola, T. & Heaton, M.M.** 2008. *A history of Nigeria.* Cambridge University Press.

174 **Romanova, V.** 2022. Ukraine's Resilience to Russia's Military Invasion in the Context of the Decentralisation Reform'. *IdeaForum: Stefan Batory Foundation.* https://www.batory.org.pl/wp-content/uploads/2022/05/Ukraines-resilience-to-Russias-military-invasion.pdf

175 **Curchoe, C.L., Chang, T.A., Trolice, M.P., Telfer, E.E., Quaas, A.M., Kearns, W.G., Stern, J.E. & Albertini, D.F.** 2022. Protecting life in a time of war. *Journal of Assisted Reproduction and Genetics,* 39(3): 555-557. https://doi.org/10.1007/s10815-022-02463-7

176 **Finlan, A.** 2021. The shape of warfare to come: a Swedish perspective 2020–2045. *Defense & Security Analysis,* 37(4): 472-491. https://doi.org/10.1080/14751798.2021.1995976

177 **Meredith, M.** 2011. *The State of Africa: A history of the continent since independence.* Simon and Schuster.

178 **Prunier, G.** 2008. *Africa's World War: Congo, the Rwandan genocide, and the making of a continental catastrophe.* Oxford University Press.

179 **Goldstein, J.S.** 2012. *Winning the war on war: The decline of armed conflict worldwide.* Penguin.

180 **Fouéré, M.-A.** 2014. Julius Nyerere, Ujamaa, and political morality in contemporary Tanzania. *African Studies Review,* 57(1): 1-24. https://doi.org/10.1017/asr.2014.3

181 **Frowein, J.A.** 1992. The Reunification of Germany. *American Journal of International Law,* 86(1): 152-163. https://doi.org/10.2307/2203146

182 **MacGregor, N.** 2014. *Germany: Memories of a nation.* Penguin UK.

183 **Wilczek, F.** 2015. Einstein's Parable of Quantum Insanity: Einstein refused to believe in the inherent unpredictability of the world. Is the subatomic world insane, or just subtle? *Quanta Magazine,* 23. https://www.scientificamerican.com/article/einstein-s-parable-of-quantum-insanity/

APPENDIXES

Appendix A: Framework for Sudan Transition

Action	Sub-Action
Immediate Actions	
1. Ending the War.	a. Instituting dispute resolution mechanisms. b. Humanitarian response to the needy and displaced persons. c. Enforcement of prohibition of unlicensed firearms. d. Peace advocacy campaign. e. Instituting potent legal deterrents to aggression. f. Banning of ideological, radical, and militarized political groups.
2. Negotiate a Peace Agreement.	a. Adoption and facilitation of an all-encompassing dialogue. b. Developing a consensus-driven framework. c. Building the foundations for trust. d. Identification and prioritization of critical issues of discord and concern. e. Drafting a comprehensive agreement. f. Enforcing and monitoring the agreement implementation.

3.	Form Agile Government of National Programs.	a.	Agreeing on a national program for transition.
		b.	Selection and vetting of the governing team.
		c.	Prioritization of accountability, transitional justice, and economic recovery.
		d.	Prioritization of institutional reforms.
		e.	Implementation of affirmative actions for post-conflict social harmony.
		f.	Prioritization of civil service reforms.
4.	Charting a Path to Elections.	a.	Establishment of an IEBC.
		b.	Setting the rules of election, electoral systems, and dispute resolution.
		c.	Securing donor funding and raising local resources to finance elections.
		d.	Census, approval of political parties, and political programs.
		e.	Establishment of election infrastructure, logistics, and technology.
		f.	Voter registration.
Intermediate Actions			
5.	Reintegrate the Armed Forces.	a.	Establishment of Armed Forces Reintegration Commission.
		b.	Agreement on a plan for collecting, controlling, and disposing of weapons.
		c.	Reviewing military capability, ranking system, and size of the armed forces.
		d.	Creation of a framework for progressive disarmament and redeployment.
		e.	Disarmament and reintegration.

6.	Secure a Process for Transitional Justice.	a.	Establishment of institutions of transitional justice.
		b.	Capacity development for transitional justice.
		c.	Securing the financial and technical support of the Sudan partners.
		d.	Developing mechanisms for widespread consultation and inclusion.
7.	Build a Resilient Peace.	a.	Securing steps to recovery and post-conflict healing.
		b.	Building resilience, adaptability, and transformation.
		c.	Building capacities to prevent or minimize future conflicts.
		d.	Promotion of social harmony.
8.	Reliable Social Infrastructure.	a.	Developing a social infrastructure plan.
		b.	Assessing infrastructure development priorities and securing funding.
		c.	Securing localized approach for better equity and ownership.
		d.	Developing national technical competencies.
		e.	Privatization and commercialization of state-owned enterprises.
		f.	Upgrading and maintenance.

Long-Term Actions		
9.	Transform the Education System.	a. Developing education vision aligned with Sudanism philosophy. b. Providing reliable illiteracy statistics. c. Developing educational infrastructure. d. Developing education plans and curricula. e. Securing funding. f. Launching education modernization and rehabilitation projects.
10.	Change Country Name and Relocate Capital City.	a. Launching public consultation. b. Assessing the pros and cons of country name change. c. Reviewing the experiences and lessons worldwide. d. Determining modalities and financial needs for the project. e. Project implementation.
11.	Abolish Tribalism.	a. Setting up the principles of Sudanism identity. b. Securing buy-in from local stakeholders. c. Drafting and approving the guiding principles. d. Advocacy and campaigning. e. Initiating practical actions toward abolishing tribalism.

12. Reintegrate the Two Sudans.	a.	Assessing the level of public support in both countries.
	b.	Assessing the economic and political merits of reintegration.
	c.	Agreeing on the principles and modalities of reintegration.
	d.	Securing political support from neighboring countries.
	e.	Prioritizing initiatives that support the long-term reintegration goal.

Appendix B: Proposed Agile Government of National Programs

Cabinet Position	Sub-Functions	Deliverables
1. First Officer	All Secretaries	1. Proper functioning of the government. 2. Reintegration of Sudan into the international community. 3. Debt forgiveness. 4. Resource mobilization.
2. Second Officer and Secretary for Foreign Affairs	First Officers cabinet, Foreign Affairs portfolio	1. Proper functioning of the government. 2. Reintegration of Sudan into the international community. 3. Debt forgiveness. 4. Resource mobilization. 5. Elections.
3. Secretary for Regular Forces and Homeland	Defense (Army), Police, Intelligence	1. Armed forces integration. 2. Development of capacity for the national police. 3. Training and military ideology. 4. Preserving the country's sovereignty.

4.	Secretary for Economy, Finance, Energy, and National Planning	Economy, Finance, and Energy, State-Owned Enterprises	1. Economic recovery. 2. International cooperation. 3. Development of resources, reforming of the tax regime, management of expenditures. 4. National planning.
5.	Secretary for National Education, Training, and Capacity Development	Education, Higher Education, Apprenticeship, Training, Capacity Development	1. Reforming the education system. 2. Capacity-building for teachers and lecturers. 3. Changing the curriculum system. 4. Improving the status of higher education. 5. Technical and scholarly exchanges with global universities. 6. Redressing scientific research.

6.	Secretary for Justice, Peace, and Social Cohesion	Transitional Justice, Employment, Youth, Women, Children, Sport, Culture, Media, Former Combatants	1. Assuring the implementation of transitional justice mechanisms. 2. Social development programs. 3. Abolition of tribalism. 4. Improving the status of youth, women, and children.
7.	Secretary of Health	Health, Medical, and Pharmaceutical Industry, Epidemiology, Social Hygiene	1. Upgrading the healthcare status. 2. Developing the healthcare industry. 3. Repatriation of Sudanese doctors.
8.	Secretary of Infrastructure and Natural Resources	Mining, Infrastructure, Water Resource Management, Agriculture, Livestock, Veterinary Services	1. Rehabilitation of social infrastructure. 2. Management of natural resources. 3. Development of the mining sector. 4. Prioritizing the agricultural sector.

9.	Governor of National Bank of Sudan	Central Bank, Commercial Banks, Financial Markets, Financial Institutions, and Financial Technology	1. Management of national currency. 2. Improving banking infrastructure. 3. Developing financial infrastructure (payment system). 4. Financial technology. 5. Reintegrating Sudanese banks into the global financial system.

Appendix C: Terms and Names Used in the Book

Term	Meaning
Abdullah Khalil	Former Prime Minister in Sudan
Abyad	Freshwater lake in South Kordofan
Agostinho Neto	MPLA leader in Angola
Al-Fasher	City in Western Sudan
Al-Idara Al-Ahlia	Arabic for Tribal Administration System
Allahu Akbar	Arabic for God is Great
Al-Sadiq Al-Mahdi	Former Prime Minister in Sudan
Arafat	Mountain in Mecca
Ariab Gold Mines	Gold mining company in Sudan
Baathis	Political Party in Sudan
Bashair	Port City in eastern Sudan
Beja	Ethnic group in eastern Sudan
Beja Congress	Resistance Movement in Sudan
Beni Aamir	Ethnic group in eastern Sudan
Damnatio ad bestias	Latin for "Condemnation to Beasts"
Daoud Yehia Bolad	Leader of Resistance Movement in Sudan
Darfur	Region in the West of Sudan
Days of Tashreeq	The three days following Eidul Adha Day
Dhul Hijjah	The twelfth month of the Islamic Calendar
Djinn	Arabic for Devil
Ee Mungu Nguvu Yetu	Kenyan National Anthem

Foday Sankoh	Leader of the Revolutionary United Front in Sierra Leone
Gacaca	Traditional Justice System in Rwanda
Al-Gadaref	City in eastern Sudan
General Abdul Aziz Al-Hilu	Leader of Resistance Movement in Sudan
General Al-Burhan	Commander of Sudan Armed Forces
General Ibrahim Abboud	Former President in Sudan
General Malik Agar	Leader of Resistance Movement in Sudan
General Numeiri	Former President in Sudan
General Suar Al-Dhahab	Former President in Sudan
Gezira	Region in Central Sudan
Hadandawa	Ethnic group in eastern Sudan
Hajj	Muslim Pilgrimage to Mecca
Harambee	Kenyan National Slogan
Hassai Gold Mines	Gold Mining Company in Sudan
Hassan Al-Turabi	Sudanese Politician
Al-Imam Al-Mahdi	Sudanese Muslim Cleric
Intifada	Arabic for Peaceful Uprising
Iqaf Sheitan Alharb	Arabic for Stopping the Devil of War
Izzatus-Sudan	Youth Military Conscription Program
Jebel Amer Gold Mines	Gold Mining Company in Sudan
Jebel Marra (Marra Mountains)	Mountains Chain in Western Sudan

John Garang	Leader of Resistance Movement in Sudan
Jonas Savimbi	Leader of UNITA Movement in Angola
Ka'bah	The Holy Mosque in Mecca
Kassala	City in eastern Sudan
Kordofan	Region in Western Sudan
Kundi	Fresh Water Lake in South Darfur
Maali Al-Wazir	An Arabic for Excellency the Minister
Malha	Saline Lake in Western Sudan
Mina	Place in Mecca
Menni Arcua Minnawi	Leader of Resistance Movement in Sudan
Musclism	Use of Muscle Power
Muthalath	Border Point between Sudan, Libya, and Chad
Muzdalifah	Place in Mecca
Nasiries	Sudanese Political Party
National Congress Party	Sudanese Political Party
National Islamic Front	Sudanese Political Party
National Unionist Party	Sudanese Political Party
Nuba Mountains	Mountains in South Kordofan
Nubians	People of Nuba Mountains
Omar Al-Bashir	Former President in Sudan
Port-Sudan	Port City in eastern Sudan
President Kagame	Rwandan President
Prime Minister Hamdok	Former Prime Minister in Sudan
Rapid Support Forces	Armed Group in Sudan

Rashaida	Ethnic group in eastern Sudan
Rashaida Free Lions	Resistance Movement in Sudan
Sawakin (or Suakin)	Port City in eastern Sudan
Sheitan (Satan)	Arabic for Devil
Shisha	Arabic for Molasse-based Tobacco
Sittat Alshai	Arabic for Tea-Selling Ladies
Sudan Liberation Movement	Resistance Movement in Darfur
Sudan People's Liberation Army/Movement	Resistance Movement in Sudan
Thamaraat	Social aid program
Tat-Heer Qabl Al-Taameer	Arabic for Clean up Before You Build
Al-Rahad	Fresh Water Lake in Kordofan
Ubuntu	Rwandan and South African National Slogan
Ujamaa	Tanzanian National Slogan
Umma Party	Sudanese Political Party
Wadi	Quasi-River
Wasta	Arabic for Favoritism
Youm Al-Nahr	Aidul Adha Day
Zaghawa	Ethnic group in Western Sudan (Darfur)

ABOUT THE AUTHOR

Eltigani Ahmed holds a PhD in organizational leadership and an M.Phil in Economics. He has over two decades of Pan-African banking experience and, in those years, led dozens of teams in creating impactful projects, facilitating multibillion-dollar deals, and growing businesses across Africa. Dr. Ahmed's interest in organizational resilience, leadership strategy, resource orchestration, and firm resource management led to a myriad of career successes as well as several publications, including groundbreaking publications in Inderscience's *International Journal of Business and Emerging Markets, International Journal of Finance & Banking Studies, International Journal of Organizational Leadership, and International Journal of Business Ecosystem & Strategy* (among others). He is also credited for proposing resource orchestration measurement inventory conjointly with other scholars. Besides his professional and writing activities, Dr. Ahmed loves discovering unfamiliar places and making new connections. He lives in Nairobi with his family.

AUTHOR PUBLICATIONS

Books

2023   Leading Resilience: Strategies for Thriving in Disruptive Times

Peer-reviewed Journal Publications

2021   An empirical assessment of the adoption and innovation of portable banking technology, *Indian* Journal *of Finance and Banking*

2021   Leadership and organizational distress: a review of the literature, International *Journal of Research in Business and Social Science*

2021   Progressive convergent definition and conceptualization of organizational resilience: A model development, *International Journal of Organizational Leadership*

2021   SME resilience to COVID-19: Insights from nonessential service providers, *International Journal of Finance & Banking Studies*

2021   The conceptualization of DROF as an anchor for organizational resilience, *International Journal of Research in Business and Social Science*

2022   Strategy-induced organizational resilience through dynamic resource orchestration, *International Journal of Research in Business and Social Science*

2022   Organizational transformation through resilience leadership strategy, *International Journal of Finance & Banking Studies*

2022   Definition, operationalization, and measurement of resilience leadership strategy, *International Journal of Organizational Leadership*

2023   Development of an inventory for the resource orchestration construct, *Inderscience Journal of Business and Emerging Markets*

2023   *Leading Resilience: Strategies for thriving in disruptive times (book – in press)*

2023   Ukraine resilience: intangible resource differential approach

2023   Development of a theory of organizational resilience constants

2023   Practical insights on the construction and empirical application of mixed methods research design

2023   The impact of systemic disruptive shocks on banking resilience